Trade and Empire in the A

Trade and Empire in the Atlantic, 1400–1600 is a book that provides an accessible and concise introduction to early European expansion overseas. It explains why and how western seafarers visited the Caribbean, South America and Africa, and looks at the history of the communities which lived around the ocean as they responded to the challenges and opportunities which sea trade opened for them.

Historical thinking on the subject of empire is naturally controversial as is shown by this survey of the first four stages of early Atlantic colonisation from the conquest of the Canary Islands to the creation of slave plantations in Brazil. This history of the Atlantic empires is an authoritative introduction to an essential topic in world history.

David Birmingham is Professor of Modern History at the University of Kent at Canterbury

Introductions to history

Edited by David Birmingham

This series of introductions to widely studied and newer areas of the undergraduate history curriculum provides short, clear, self-contained and incisive guides for the student reader.

Introductions to History

Series Editor: David Birmingham
Professor of Modern History, University of Kent at Canterbury

A series initiated by members of the School of History at the University of Kent at Canterbury

Trade and Empire in the Atlantic, 1400–1600

David Birmingham

London and New York

First published 2000
by Routledge
11 New Fetter Lane, London EC4P 4EE

Simultaneously published in the USA and Canada
by Routledge
29 West 35th Street, New York, NY 10001

Routledge is an imprint of the Taylor & Francis Group

© 2000 David Birmingham

Typeset in Sabon and Gill Sans by
J&L Composition Ltd, Filey, North Yorkshire
Printed and bound in Great Britain by MPG Books Ltd, Bodmin

British Library Cataloguing in Publication Data
A catalogue record for this book is available from the British Library

Library of Congress Cataloging in Publication Data
Birmingham, David
    The Atlantic empires, 1400–1600/David Birmingham.
       p. cm – (Introductions to history)
    Includes bibliographical references and index.
    1. Colonies – History.   2. Europe – Colonies – History.   I. Title.
    II. Series.
JV125.B57 2000
325'.32'091821 – dc21   99–058424

ISBN 0–415–23460–3 (hbk)
ISBN 0–415–23206–6 (pbk)

Contents

Maps

Introduction

The literature of empire falls into two categories, the romantic and the academic. The romantic literature has focused on the magical names of Henry the Navigator and Christopher Columbus and has been embroidered with legend and enhanced by patriotism. The academic literature has explored the complex interactions between different peoples on four continents. In the works of the new scholars the primacy of Europe has been toned down in favour of a closer look at other cultures on other shores. The rigid vision of an Old World divided between the faiths of Islam and Christendom by a sort of 'cold war' has been softened by a new awareness of co-operation, as well as conflict, between peoples of different beliefs and traditions. In place of adventure as a primary theme, more attention has been given to commerce in the history of the Atlantic.

The old heroes, or anti-heroes, of the early Atlantic still have their place in history since they epitomise the activities of the many sailors and financiers from Italy and from Flanders, as well as from Spain and Portugal, who were pioneers in the colonial empires of the tropics. Columbus was a cloth merchant from Genoa who belonged to an integrated web of Italian traders from the western Mediterranean, many of whom had settled in the Atlantic ports of Lisbon and Seville. Henry was a royal prince of Portugal, a grandson of the great English warrior John of Gaunt, and as a very young soldier he took part in a famous raid across the 'Pillars of Hercules' into Africa. Both men were children of their time and both received a mixed reception at the hands of historians. The reputation of Columbus peaked in 1892, the quatercentenary of his ocean crossing, before the white peoples of the New World had grasped the scale of the devastation that he had brought in his wake. Henry's reputation lasted half a century longer, and in 1960, five hundred years after he died, Portugal raised a monument to his memory while still clinging to an empire in Africa.

The early history of the Atlantic, between 1400 and 1600, developed in four stages. The island stage saw immigrants settling on Madeira, the Canaries and other islands, bringing with them their crops and their animals and producing wheat and sugar, planting cotton and woad, preparing sheep's wool and cattle hides, and pioneering the ideas of overseas empire. The second phase of colonial enterprise related to the mainland of Africa as merchant adventurers began to trade in salt, textiles and gold. They also established diplomatic and religious links with several of the old kingdoms of Africa. A dramatic third stage of European overseas expansion carried the pioneers and the merchants clear across the Atlantic to land on the Caribbean islands. Twenty-five years later they used these islands as the base from which to conquer the great North American empire of Mexico. A generation later immigrants from Spain discovered a rich vein of silver and added mining to the colonial traditions of planting and ranching. By 1600 250,000 migrants from Spain had settled in the American uplands and had founded some 200 colonial towns. The fourth and final stage in old-style colonisation brought settlers and missionaries to the southern hemisphere where they conquered and converted Brazil on one side of Atlantic and Angola on the other. It was in the south that a system of plantations worked by slaves was devised and by 1600 the colonisers of the New World had bought 100,000 slaves in Africa and cruelly carried them into an exile filled with hard labour and devoid of all freedom. Over the next three centuries 10 million African slaves were to be carried to the Americas to replace Native American peoples who had died as the result of foreign colonisation.

The principal question to which each and every historian must seek his or her own set of answers is why did Europe's colonial pioneers reach out so far into the Atlantic in the fifteenth and sixteenth centuries? One answer must be that poverty was the spur. Genoese merchants on a narrow shoreline hemmed in by mountains, or Portuguese noblemen deprived of fertile land, had to reach out beyond the home territory to fulfil their aspirations. It can be argued, to dramatise the matter, that the price of bread in the city of Lisbon was the single most important factor in launching the age of empire. But if poverty was one spur, the other was wealth. The spice merchants of Flanders and the silk vendors of Andalucia sought to outflank their rich Levantine trading partners in Syria and Egypt by finding Atlantic sea-lanes to

India and China. The Atlantic route to China eventually had to cross the unexpected barrier of Central America, while the one to India had to head south to round the Cape of Africa. By 1600 both the eastern and the western sea routes from Europe to Asia were flourishing, but the Atlantic was far more than a maritime alternative to the Persian silk caravans and the Arab spice convoys. This book is about the communities that lived around the ocean and the ways in which they responded to the opportunities and challenges opened up by sea trade. Although farming and ranching took pride of place in the Atlantic world, it will be shown how the European thirst for gold, and later for silver, modified the ancient politics of mining in Africa and the Americas.

This study is not based on any original research. Instead it owes a huge debt to the many scholars who have personally explored the thousands of archival files that reveal the history of the the old colonial system in the Atlantic. Several of those scholars are listed at the end of this book and I am very grateful to all of them. They have been my companions as I tried to create a word-picture of the Atlantic over the two centuries that followed the closing of the middle ages. As the publisher's reader rightly pointed out, this is little more than a pamphlet-sized introduction to the subject and a bigger and better book would have devoted more space to administrative history, military history and the changes which colonial activities brought to the imperial homelands. Presented here is my own selective picture, and it arises from questions I have tried to ask as a modern historian looking back to the origins of the colonial empires. The end of empire, and the decolonisation of Africa, is a topic I have dealt with in a book previously published in this series.

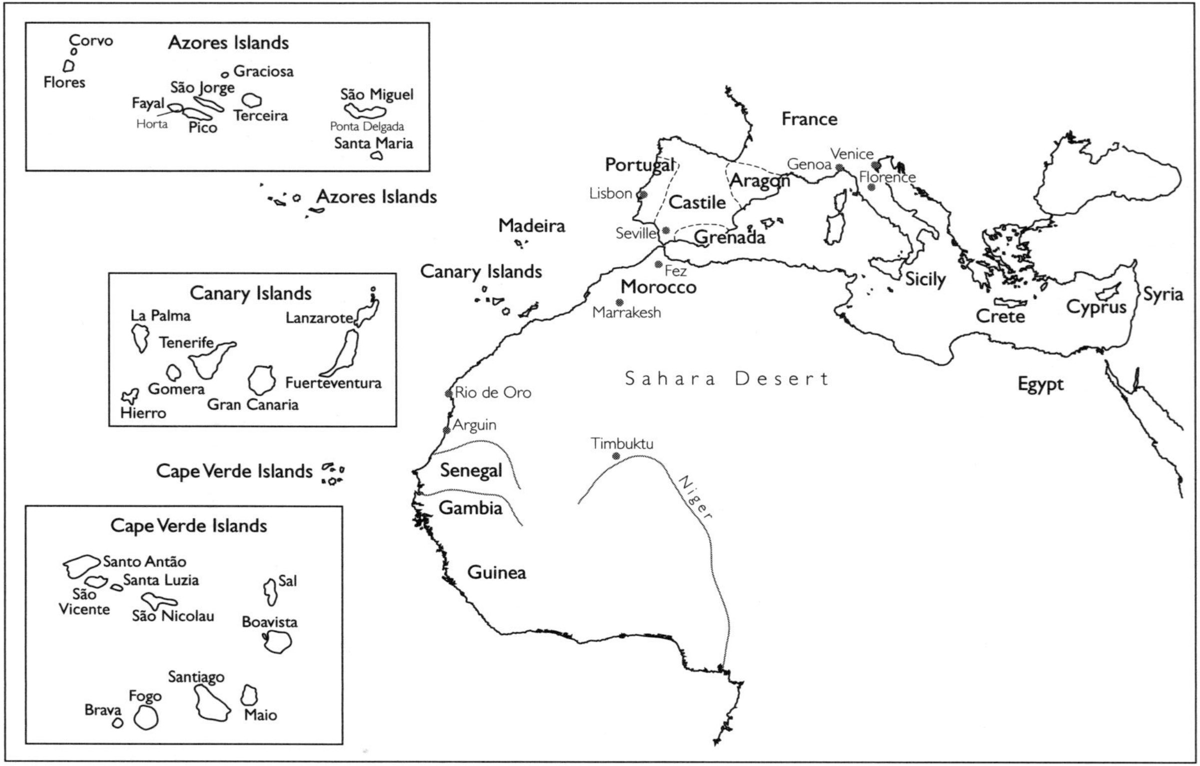

Map 1 The Atlantic islands

CHAPTER ONE

Colonising the Atlantic islands

The ideas and techniques of colonisation used by Europeans who settled foreign lands were often pioneered on islands. Some of these islands were uninhabited, as was Iceland when the Vikings began to settle there in the tenth century. Others were already peopled, as was Ireland when Norman colonisers introduced themselves by force of arms in the twelfth century. In the fifteenth century the inhabited Atlantic islands colonised by Spain were the Canary Islands off the coast of Africa and later the Caribbean islands off the coast of America. At the same time, or even a little earlier, the Portuguese developed their colonising experiences on Atlantic islands that were not inhabited, Madeira and the Azores in the temperate zone, and the Cape Verdes and São Tomé in the tropics. As both Spain and Portugal stretched out from their home shores they learnt much about the economics of colonisation from the experiences of Genoa and Venice, the great merchant republics of Italy that had grown wealthy on colonial trade with the islands of the Mediterranean and the shores of the Black Sea. They also gained the new skills needed to venture out into the Atlantic through close contact with the seafaring peoples of the Netherlands who purchased the new colonial produce and supplied fine manufactures in return. Although the Portuguese became the great merchants of Africa, and the Spaniards became the great settlers of America, an important financial role was also played by Europe's largest and wealthiest cities in Italy and the Netherlands. Together the merchants, emigrants, sailors and bankers of Europe played key roles in planting their concepts of production and exchange among the peoples of the Atlantic world. In 1400 this tropical world was scarcely known to Europe. By 1600 an Atlantic system of colonial trade and migration was fully functioning as peoples, plants and produce flowed along new sea-lanes.

In 1420 the first successful step was taken in the modern colonising of the Atlantic. The island of Madeira, 600 miles off the coast of Portugal and 400 miles from Morocco, was claimed by two conquerors who partitioned it between themselves. The northern and eastern half of the island was granted by a Portuguese royal charter of donation to Tristão Vaz, a cavalryman who had failed to make his fortune in the Christian raids on the Islamic mainland of Morocco and instead took a lease on half of the uninhabited, and previously neglected, offshore island. The southern and western half of Madeira was granted by donation to João Gonçalves, another lesser nobleman of Portugal with some experience of seaborne warfare. In addition to the two aristocratic claimants a third proprietor took possession of the small island of Porto Santo, off the north coast of Madeira. He was Bartholomew Perestrello, a middle-class member of Portugal's influential community of Italian merchants. It was from among these Luso-Italians that the peripatetic court of Portugal had often appointed harbour officials to manage the trade of Lisbon. Thus it was that the court and the Italians played an early role in financing and staffing the Portuguese colonial ventures.

The new lords-proprietor of Madeira did not 'discover' the islands which they claimed in 1420. Their existence and approximate location had been known to seafarers, particularly Genoese seafarers, for a century or more. Any fourteenth-century adventurer sailing down the coast of Africa, and then wanting to find the best winds and currents to return to Europe or the Mediterranean, was quite likely to sail far enough offshore to sight Madeira. According to legend, one such merchant mariner was Robert Machin of Bristol who lived on Madeira after being shipwrecked there. His tale was told by members of his crew who paddled their way to the mainland and were eventually ransomed from Morocco and returned to Christian Europe. Machin's name may survive in corrupted form as Machico, later to be the capital town of the eastern half of Madeira. Whether true or false, the legend symbolises real Atlantic experience and casual visitors from Catalonia, Normandy and elsewhere probably stopped quite regularly at Madeira to obtain fresh water and firewood for the galleys on their ships.

The formal colonisation of Madeira after 1420 did not immediately provide the new owners with wealth. On the contrary, making a profit from a rugged and heavily wooded land which had no indigenous people was a struggle. Foraging was the first economic activity and one of the few viable products was resin from the great trees of the virgin forest, a resin colloquially known as 'dragon's blood' and sold to the weaving and dyeing industries of Europe for stiffening materials. A more important, if less picturesque, source of revenue was the wood itself, the product from which the island gained its name: Legname on early Italian charts or Madeira in Portuguese. Portugal was short of good timber and had to import its ships' timbers from the Baltic at considerable expense. In addition to supplying shipyards, Madeira also furnished roofing timbers of such quality that the old Arab styles of roofing in Lisbon began to be replaced by wide tiled roofs supported on long beams. Although Madeira developed a logging industry, the extraction process was wasteful and many of Madeira's great trees were not sawn up for export but simply burnt by settlers seeking farm land. Timber merchants had limited means of transport and much of the island was surrounded by cliffs without beaches suitable for loading ships. Settlers soon turned their hand from logging to agriculture.

The colonial farmers who settled on Madeira experimented initially with the growing of wheat. In later centuries the planting of wheat was to become one of the important activities of colonial settlers around the world when prairies were ploughed and great sailing clippers raced each other through the Atlantic to reach the European markets ahead of their rivals. The earliest precursors of these grain merchants supplied the Lisbon market by undercutting the price of Spanish corn from the neighbouring kingdom of Castile. Portugal had regularly needed to import one-fifth of its cereal requirements since three-quarters of the country's arable land was barely cultivated. A lack of navigable rivers or cart tracks meant that it was cheaper to ferry wheat from islands out in the Atlantic than to bring it from the dusty and thinly peopled inland farms on the plains of the interior. The fertile soils of the islands, catching the wet Atlantic winds as they did, were nearly twice as productive as those on the Portuguese mainland.

The Madeira wheat farmers might have been more successful if they had not brought with them rabbits who soon escaped from their farmyard hutches and took to the wild, doing extensive damage to the crops that peasants sowed. Despite such hazards, wheat initially grew quite well on the newly cleared soils and the harvest sold profitably back in Europe. It can be argued that regular shortages of bread in the harbour-city of Lisbon had been one of the more important, if mundane, driving forces behind Portuguese overseas colonisation. In particular Lisbon had been seriously short of bread flour in 1414 when wheat shipments coming from Flanders and England had been diverted to Morocco where a poor harvest had temporarily made corn prices very attractive. To the Lisbon city fathers the prospect of 'home-grown' wheat, cultivated on Madeira by Portuguese peasants, and shipped by Portuguese boatmen, was an attractive alternative to foreign supplies that were subject to economic, climatic and political disruption. But although the Madeira captaincies sold some wheat to Lisbon, and occasionally even to Morocco, cereal production did not flourish. After 1450 it was the Azores Islands, further out into the ocean, which provided Portugal with island wheat. By the sixteenth century the Azores shipped some 400,000 bushels of wheat to Portugal each year. Madeira, meanwhile, moved on to a different economic plane and successfully adopted sugar cultivation.

Sugar cane was originally a succulent grass that became a 'spice' crop in both India and China during the first millennium AD. By the middle ages cane was being grown, and sugar was being pressed and purified, in Egypt and Syria before it became a Mediterranean crop on the islands of both Cyprus and Crete. From there it was introduced to Muslim plantations on the island of Sicily and in southern Spain. Christian merchants bought small quantities of sugar as an expensive luxury, or as a medicinal comfort, but it was only a sideline in their daily dealings with their trans-Mediterranean trade partners. The most westerly of the Muslim estates were in the Algarve, a kingdom conquered by Christian invaders in 1249 and thereafter permanently linked to the crown of Portugal. It was from the Algarve that the royal family of Portugal, with its distinctly non-aristocratic interest in trade, began to explore opportunities for sugar planting on the Atlantic islands.

In the 1450s, after thirty years of semi-successful foraging, logging and wheat gardening, the lords-proprietor of Madeira surrendered the colonial initiative to the Portuguese royal princes. The island was thereafter radically transformed politically, economically and techno-logically by the introduction of sugar cane. The quasi-revolutionary change from cereal farming to sugar milling created an economic model that was later to be adopted throughout much of the Atlantic world. The agents of the entrepreneurial princes apparently brought high-quality sugar-cane roots from Sicily, but obtaining a good strain of cane was only the first step in developing a new industry. Sugar production also required a considerable input of capital and technology. This the royal princes were little more willing or able to supply than had been the aristocratic captains whom they supplanted. They therefore approached Portugal's semi-foreign 'bourgeoisie' for help and turned in particular to the Genoese community of Luso-Italians who had dominated so much of the mercantile life of Portugal in the two centuries since Christians had conquered the land. Italians provided the finance, the technology and the shipping for early Atlantic colonisation while the Portuguese provided the workforce.

The establishment of a sugar plantation required an extensive labour force. Men, women and children were needed to clear the land, till the soil, plant the canes and cut the crop when it reached maturity. During the the harvest the cane had to be processed rapidly before the juice in the sugar stem began to dry out. In favourable circumstances porters could use carts or canoes. Normally, however, they loaded the huge bundles on their backs and worked gruelling hours to carry the cane to the crushing mill. On Madeira most harvest workers were family members or hired immigrant labourers from Europe. The supply of willing migrant labour, however, was initially neither adequate nor reliable. For fifteenth-century Portuguese workers the idea of emigration was not the obvious escape route from poverty that it became in later centuries, since by 1450 Portugal had barely reached the population levels that had prevailed before the arrival of the Black Death. Portugal remained quite sparsely peopled and its landowners were reluctant to see their labourers leave the home soil to seek fortune in the infant colony out in the ocean. Early colonial migrants, like later ones, were often those who shifted as best they could on society's margins, some of them malefactors who preferred emigration to serving a term of hard labour in prison. Even when the poor, the landless and a few criminals had offered their services there were still not enough labourers from Portugal to expand the Madeira sugar industry. In these circumstances some farmers pioneered a new labour policy by supplementing their workforce with one or two purchased slaves, a practice still normal at the time in southern Spain and Portugal where slaves were usually conquered and converted Muslims.

Slavery was to become a key institution in the development of the sugar industry of the early modern colonies both in the Old World and in the New American one. In Madeira slavery was theoretically viable but it was a costly labour option. It was viable because the island was relatively small and slaves who escaped into the hills from their harsh and unrewarding servitude were likely to be recaptured and chastised. But slaves were expensive. Early sugar planters bought some of their slaves from the Canary Islands off the south coast of Morocco. They had to pay the slave raiders the cost of their military actions as well as the capital depreciation on their ships. The wages of the crews which brought the live 'cargoes' to Madeira, and the rewards appropriate to the captains who managed the whole violent business, also added to the price of each slave. Despite the high risks, Italian ship owners took a prominent part in the early slave-carrying business. With encouragement from the Portuguese royal princes, new sources of supply were gradually investigated. Portuguese, Genoese and a few Venetian robber-captains began to visit the African shore south of the Canaries. When lucky they were able able to round up and capture unsuspecting victims whom they carried off as slaves.

One of the first Portuguese slave raids into sub-Saharan Africa was undertaken by a relative of João Gonçalves, the original lord-proprietor of Madeira. Young António Gonçalves was a page-boy in the service of Prince Henry and, despite the lad's youth, the prince appointed him to serve on a small caravel that had been fitted out for a deep raid into the African tropics in about 1443. The wild young men of the prince's household sailed beyond the most arid section of the Saharan coast and landed by night. At dawn they saw a column of water-carriers heading to a desert-side well. Seizing their weapons, they fell upon them, scattering the majority but capturing thirteen men and women. Some of their prizes were of a reddish colour but others were black-skinned. The captain of the expedition was so pleased with the exploit that the young António was recommended for a knighthood for the daring leadership he had shown during the raid. Back in Portugal Prince Henry was equally delighted with the lucrative, if inhuman, outcome of the venture.

Few of the slaves who were captured, purchased or bartered on the African coast went to Madeira. Most of them were either kept in Portugal or sold to southern Spain. Although some Africans did work on the Madeira sugar farms and in the mills, black people did not become a lasting slave caste or a distinctive racial group on the island. As in Portugal itself, where much larger numbers of black Africans worked on the farms and in some domestic sectors in the towns, the immigrants from Africa were steadily absorbed into the wider homogenised island population. Labour on the sugar fields, even slave labour, was essentially an extension of the traditional form of

Portuguese farm labour in which workers were subservient family clients expected to turn their hand to all domestic or field work. Despite the cosmopolitan additions to its society, Madeira became and remained a Portuguese-speaking colony of white Roman Catholics.

Next to the labour force a second requirement of a successful sugar farm was an adequate supply of water. Where rainfall was adequate – as in many of the tropical plantations later established around the Atlantic – the cost of preserving water was not a significant contributor to success or failure. In Madeira, however, rainfall was seasonal and regional. The volcanic rock acted like a giant sponge that absorbed water in winter and fed the springs in summer. In order to grow sugar on the most favourable southern slopes it was necessary to build an expensive system of irrigation. Canals channelled out of the hillside, or even carved along cliff faces, brought water from springs to the most fertile agricultural terraces. Some channels ran for miles and had to be carefully maintained, to repair damage, and patrolled, to prevent pilferage and ensure that water was only taken from the sluices by those entitled to it. In later centuries engineers were able to cut tunnels through mountains to bring water across the island from the wetter northern slopes to the warmer southern slopes. To make the best use of the watered topsoil, many miles of terrace walls were built on the sunny side of the island.

Water was required on Madeira not only for irrigation but as a source of energy. One of the technological revolutions of Atlantic history was the introduction of the water wheel. This expensive but efficient substitute for animal and human labour was adopted on Madeira wherever the water supply was adequate. On large farms the treadmills worked by labourers, and the yoke mills turned by oxen, were replaced by watermills that could ceaselessly turn the crushing wheels of the sugar mills night and day. The cost of building a large watermill was beyond the reach of any peasant, and the sugar industry gradually came to be dominated by entrepreneurs with access to investment capital. Over time the speculators built a hundred mills on Madeira. Many of the sugar producers who supplied these mills, or invested in them, were neither noblemen nor farmers but members of the professional and artisan classes: cobblers, barbers, surgeons, stonemasons, carpenters or even members of the clergy. Mill owners crushed not only their own sugar, but the cane which their small-scale peasant neighbours brought to them for contract processing. Wherever possible they used water for energy since oxen were expensive to buy and had to be fed on hay that competed for land usage with the sugar crop itself. Maintaining the mills, however, was a skilled and expensive business. The specialised carpenters who came to Madeira to build and and maintain the water wheels were of such crucial importance to the island economy that all mill-owners constantly feared that craftsmen might emigrate to the African mainland to work in the flourishing sugar mills in the valleys of southern Morocco. Attempted flight by skilled artisans was made a punishable offence on Madeira.

One key to success in the sugar industry was the process used for purification. The first sugar growers allegedly dried their cane juice in the sun. It was later realised that to obtain better sugar it was necessary to heat the fresh juice artificially over a fire. The resulting molasses was heated again to obtain the best qualities of both white and brown sugar. An Italian witness, Julius Landi, provided a detailed account of the process. When the cane was crushed between wooden rollers the sap was collected in wooden tubs and then heated at five different temperatures in five successive metal vats. Impurities and froth were skimmed off from the first boiling and turned into the coarse rum-like alcohol that later became a famous item of barter in the African slave trade. The sugar passed through several more stages of heating, stirring, beating, filtering and moulding before being sold as seven different categories of sugar whose prices ranged from 220 to 530 reales per quarter-hundredweight. To undertake this refining it was necessary to make and maintain expensive metal boiling vats. Madeira had no mines of its own and therefore iron, tin and copper had to be bought from abroad. The skilled coppersmiths, tinsmiths and blacksmiths who made and repaired the sugar cauldrons were immigrants who could demand privileged wages. At the other end of the employment scale unskilled labourers had to cut, haul and stack huge supplies of firewood for the processing plant. Wood had to be collected and stored throughout the year so that the vats could be kept boiling during the harvest season. Heavy bundles of firewood increasingly had to be brought from many miles away as the supply of trees receded and the land planted with sugar expanded.

Despite the problems of obtaining skills and investments the Madeira sugar industry flourished for a hundred years and provided the industrial model for later plantation societies devoted to sugar. The Venetian chronicler Alvise Cadamosto reported that by 1455 the infant industry was already producing twenty tons of sugar per year. Fifteen years later the sugar exports had risen twentyfold, and by the end of the fifteenth century annual production probably exceeded 1,500 tons. By now the Portuguese crown had replaced the semi-autonomous princes as the driving force of empire and it had a deep financial interest in the industry. In 1505 King Manuel of Portugal claimed that Martim de Almeida, the contractor to whom Madeira's taxes had been farmed out, owned him 600 tons of sugar. Production remained high for another half-century, but thereafter Madeira declined, soils became exhausted, erosion was not adequately stemmed, firewood became scarce, and newer, larger plantations in the South Atlantic began to offer stiff competition.

During its century of pre-eminence Madeira had created a market for Atlantic sugar that was to grow almost without limit for several centuries. Only a small proportion of what was produced went to Portugal. This modest scale of Portuguese imports reflected the relative poverty of a country in which the average consumption of sugar, at the end of the fifteenth century, was only three ounces per person per year. This average, however, was not evenly distributed and young people at the princely courts enjoyed receiving gifts of sugar at their Christmas festivities. A century later the dowager queen of Portugal and her ladies-in-waiting were particularly addicted to the candied fruits that were made with Madeira sugar. In the winter of 1571 the queen received ninety-seven small barrels of sweetmeats including sugared peaches, plums, pears, oranges, and candied lemon peel. The gourmets of France also appreciated the sugar-candy of Madeira. The most important customers for Madeira sugar, however, were the wholesale grocers of Flanders, in the southern Netherlands. Antwerp was one of the richest ports of Europe and its traders were well connected in all the main cities around the North Sea and the Baltic as well as in many riverside markets of the German hinterland. At least a quarter of Madeira's sugar went to Flanders, some six times more than was sent to Portugal itself.

Although the lion's share of Madeira's sugar went to Flanders, a small quantity was also sent to England and a consignment of about a hundred tons was refined each year in Bristol, which was later to become England's leading sugar port. A rather more important destination for Atlantic sugar than England, despite the competing supplies from the local Mediterranean sugar industries, was Italy. Venice, once a great sugar port of the Middle East, now imported sugar from Madeira and re-exported it as far afield as Constantinople.

In the western Mediterranean the city-republic of Genoa supplemented its local supplies by importing twice as much Madeira sugar as either Portugal or England, and one of the many Italians involved in this trade was Christopher Columbus. In 1478 the young Columbus was commissioned by two Italian wholesalers to buy sugar on Madeira. His venture was far from successful when the Flemish dealer Jean de Esmerault refused to accept the cloth he had to sell and Columbus was stranded for three years on the island, taking refuge in the house of the Italian Perestrello family which owned the small neighbouring island of Porto Santo. During the long wait for his fortunes to improve, Columbus married one of the Perestrello daughters and his son Diego was born on Madeira.

Madeira was not the only Atlantic island to be colonised in the midfifteenth century by settlers from Portugal, financiers from Italy and merchants from Flanders. A thousand miles out into the ocean lay the Azores, whose volcanic soils were not markedly different from those of Madeira but whose climate was wetter and cooler. This made the introduction of colonial sugar as a cash crop slower and more precarious. So slow was the development of the industry, and so limited the investment in mills, that sugar planters on the island of Santa Maria had to take their cut cane across to the island of São Miguel to have it processed. Fifty years after the first settlers had began to clear their plots they were still struggling to produce fifty tons of sugar between them and by 1520 their yield of 200 tons was little more than a tenth of Madeira's. Rather than competing with warmer islands to grow sugar, the Azores settlers tried to make their living from other agricultural and commercial activities.

One exotic crop that was grown on the Azores for nearly two centuries was woad. The blue dye that was extracted from the plant was particularly valued in the sixteenth century before being supplanted by another colonial dye crop, indigo, which rival colonies later produced more economically and in greater volume. At the peak of production the Azores industry was selling 60,000 bales of cured dye leaves a year to the textile markets of Flanders, France and England. The processing of woad, like the refining of sugar, was an intensive business that required much labour and time. The dried leaves had to be crushed, wetted and ground several times over before being made into hundredweight bales ready for export. Each bale of dyestuff required 2,000 pounds-weight of green leaves and in the late sixteenth century the island of São Miguel may have devoted more than a third of its arable land to woad before the trade dwindled and then vanished.

In addition to practising agriculture the Azores developed service industries and became a way-station for ships returning from the New World. Christopher Columbus unexpectedly, and possibly unintentionally, called at the Azores in 1492 on his tattered return from the first European voyage to the Caribbean. The island of Horta was later described as 'the greatest entrepôt, emporium, and victualling and fuelling station between Europe and North America' (Bentley Duncan, 1972: 137). The town of Horta, which was given municipal status in 1498, later came to host the cod fleets returning from Newfoundland and the sugar fleets coming up from South America. Despite the economic importance and strategic location of Horta harbour, Sir Walter Raleigh was disappointed with his spoils when he plundered the town in 1597. His men had to content themselves with looting four churches that they then burnt down. A hundred years after this outrage the harbour was regularly and peacefully visited by scores of English ships each year as they plied their way back from New England to the mother country. In addition to providing shelter, water and repairs for long-range Atlantic shipping, the Azores began to produce wine that could be supplied for onboard consumption by ships' crews or for resale in other colonies.

The Portuguese control of the Azores was modelled on their control of Madeira. Indeed, the donation charter for the island of São Miguel was held by the Gonçalves family, which had provided the first lord-proprietor of Madeira and whose son had pioneered one of the early slave raids to West Africa. In 1580 the seventh hereditary holder of the captaincy of São Miguel, and the head of the Azores branch of the family, was ennobled with the rank of earl. In the same year the island of Terceira hosted the exiled claimant to the Portuguese throne, Prince António, but his claim was abortive and the Spanish Habsburgs captured the Azores, along with the rest of the Portuguese empire. Spain fortified the island with a gigantic mid-Atlantic fortress, named after Philip II, which was designed to protect the transatlantic fleets from Mexico rather than defend the agricultural and service economies of the islands. Although the Azores remained important for those who wanted rescue and repair in mid-Atlantic, they were virtually forgotten by the rest of the world and their peasants quietly cultivated their fields of wheat and vines without making any major innovative contribution to the concepts of colonisation that were being explored on other Atlantic islands, such as the Canaries.

The Canary Islands were the third set of Atlantic islands on which Europe pioneered its experiments in overseas colonisation. Although the islands provided opportunities for growing wheat, sugar and wine, their history was in some respects remarkably different from that of Madeira and the Azores. In particular the Canary Islands were not uninhabited but had their own indigenous population with its own indigenous culture. The islands were almost within sight of the African mainland, but they had remained independent of successive Moroccan empires. Since antiquity foreigners, be they Phoenicians, Romans, Muslims or Iberians, had rarely if ever cared to settle there, though they sometimes raided the people for slave labour. The first regular visitors to the Canary Islands were Italians. A Florentine from Lisbon made a report in 1341 and a Genoese from Seville lived on Lanzarote in 1365 and gave the island his name. By 1382 Castilians were also regular traders in the islands where they bought slaves for the farms of southern Spain. Foragers also came looking for resins and dyes for the textile industry. They found that orchilla lichens, which gave a deep purple colour, were a particularly valuable wild plant. Rather more numerous than the gatherers were the French shepherds who brought their flocks and herds by sea to graze on the dry outer islands where local goatherds offered only limited resistance to immigrant rivals. In 1402 militant invaders from Normandy began the first of many campaigns to conquer the more fertile central islands. The Norman leader Jean de Béthencourt claimed the title of 'king' of the Canaries and appointed his nephew as the governor. He even persuaded the pope to appoint a bishop for his islands, but his colonisation had only limited success and the Norman conquerors 'sold' their shaky claim to Prince Henry of Portugal. In 1448 the Portuguese began to activate this dormant claim and even tried to impose taxes on Canary Island settlers. They were driven off, however, by Castilians from Spain who had gained an equally precarious claim to the islands. In 1479 the periodic assertions of sovereignty by Portugal and Spain were finally settled by the Treaty of Alcaçovas which left the Canaries to Spain but gave all the other islands to Portugal.

The Canary island of Tenerife bore some similarity to Madeira. It was high and volcanic and the dry land was suitable for wheat cultivation while the wetter slopes were ideal for sugar. The early immigrants were predominantly Portuguese, some of them moving south from

Madeira in search of vacant lands. They brought their cultivation techniques and engineering skills, particularly in irrigation. It was the sugar farmers on the wet land, and not the wheat farmers on the dry, who made good money on the Canary Islands and became the landed élite. While the Portuguese undertook the hard labour, dug the irrigation canals and managed the plantations, Genoese capitalists built the mills and marketed the refined sugar. Many of these Italians belonged to the large community of Genoese expatriates that had long been settled in Seville, Castile's leading port with river access to the Atlantic down the Guadalquivir River. In addition to Portuguese and Italians, Castilians from south-western Spain also came to Tenerife, many of them newly converted Muslims and Jews who had been banned from practising their ancestral religions in Spain and forced to accept Christianity. From the Canaries it was sometimes possible for Spanish 'New Christians' to visit Morocco and attend Friday prayers at a mosque, or visit a synagogue on the Sabbath. The Canary branch of the Inquisition naturally took a hostile view of such practices and was constantly on the lookout for the survival of Islamic and Judaic ritual and belief in the colonies. For those who had sailed to the colonies seeking opportunities for clandestine worship, Marrakesh in Morocco was a much more open metropolitan city than any in Iberia and illicit relations with Morocco were a significant part of Canary Island culture and commerce.

Tenerife, like Madeira, was initially granted by charter of donation to a captain-general who was appointed to rule over it. Alonso de Lugo was the first of the great Spanish conquistadores of the Atlantic empires and his career set the pattern for later private initiatives in the conquest of foreign lands. De Lugo had first made his money as a sugar planter on the island of Gran Canaria where he built a sugar mill in 1484. When he decided to attempt the conquest of Tenerife he sold his mill to finance the recruitment of his army of invaders. Although the principalities of the Guanche-speaking chiefs on Tenerife put up fierce resistance to the invaders, they were no match for the better-armed conquistadores and within ten years most had been driven out of the fertile north and forced to seek refuge as pastoralists in the arid south of the island. In the north many Canarians who survived the military action were later killed by the spread of plague. Throughout the campaigns men and women who resisted the invaders were captured and taken into slavery, either to work on new Castilian estates or to be sold into exile in Madeira or Spain. Although many Canarians suffered oppression and death during the conquest, a few were assimilated into the new, Hispanicised, colonial society. The colonial population of Tenerife was made up in roughly equal proportions of Portuguese, Castilians and native Canarians. Some of the old chiefs who were absorbed into the new society were granted a colonial status appropriate to their rank. A few members of this indigenous élite remained wealthy landowners and even married into the colonial high society of the Norman Béthencourts or the Castilian noble family of Medina Sidonia.

Parcelling out land naturally caused rivalry and jealousy among the Canary Island invaders. On Tenerife Alonso de Lugo was accused of neglecting the claims of true Castilians in favour of 'foreigners' – Portuguese and Italians – who were dependent on his largesse for their success. Although not as numerous as the Portuguese immigrant community, Italians remained prominent throughout the islands and several of their sugar mills were assessed at more than one thousand gold ducats each. On Tenerife the sugar mills reached a capacity of one thousand tons of sugar a year by the early sixteenth century and almost matched the Madeira sugar industry for size. To keep the mills working, and expand the estates, the new proprietors had to win an ever larger supply of fresh labour. The local Canarian population was deemed by legal custom to be segregated between the 'peaceable natives' and those branded the 'warrior tribes'. The crown of Castile decreed it legitimate to attack and enslave 'warrior tribes'. All too often, however, not enough captives could be secured under this dispensation and Alonso de Lugo and his retainers showed little compunction in rounding up additional slaves among the 'peaceable' peoples. Worse still the defeated peoples were not allocated to conquistadores, like serfs attached to their land, but were considered a separate and distinct form of war booty whose owners were at liberty to sell them as captives to the highest bidder at home or abroad.

The island of Gran Canaria had a colonial history slightly different to that of Tenerife. Instead of being conquered by a quasi-autonomous warlord, Gran Canaria was ruled by a military 'governor' appointed by the Castilian crown. Whereas Tenerife had been conquered by an independent military commander at his own expense, Gran Canaria was conquered on behalf of the crown of Castile and at least partly at royal expense. On the island the post of governor was closely supervised, and new holders of the office were regularly appointed. On Tenerife Alonso de Lugo was lord-proprietor for life and enjoyed his status and his wealth until his death in 1525. On Gran Canaria the powers of the governor were circumscribed not only by the edicts of the crown, but by an administrative council of influential citizens. Although municipal towns in the Canaries did not acquire the affluence and influence that they had previously enjoyed in Spain, some colonial wealth was ploughed back into civic architecture and town residences. With the bureaucratisation of the Spanish empire colonial careers could be won as bureaucrats rather than as planters and some educated immigrants settled in the towns. Urban centres were to be important features of both Portuguese and Spanish Atlantic societies, but in the Canaries they remained essentially modest. The Canaries, like the Azores, became a staging post on the long haul to and from America and it was the minor trades which survived, supplying wood and pitch for ship repairs, cheese and fish for colonial provisions, hides and skins for the leather industry, and money laundering for pirates who preyed on the Atlantic economy.

A thousand miles south of the Canaries a fourth set of islands presented the Atlantic colonisers with new challenges and opportunities. The Cape Verde Islands were 300 miles off the African shore and therefore had not been seen by early coastal sailors. The first known visitor was Antonio da Noli, who came from Genoa and described the islands in 1455. Soon afterwards the Venetian chronicler Cadamosto, already familiar with Madeira and the Canaries, visited the Cape Verdes. Three years later Diogo Gomes of Portugal reached the islands and challenged the colonial claims of Antonio da Noli, who had been made the lord-proprietor of the southern half of the island of Santiago. In 1461, after Prince Fernando of Portugal had inherited the colonial enterprises of Prince Henry, the smaller of the Cape Verde Islands were explored and the northern half of Santiago was awarded to a Portuguese lord-proprietor.

The colonisation of the Cape Verdes was slow to take root. Genoa could supply ships and seamen, but Portugal could not provide willing settlers since the soils were less obviously suited to sugar-growing than those of Madeira or Tenerife. Despite the poor prospects, Antonio da Noli's family did manage to plant sugar using slave workers from the African mainland. At the same time two Castilians, namesakes of Alonso de Lugo, the conquistador of Tenerife, began to gather orchilla lichens for dyestuff, as had been done by early visitors to the Canaries. In the late 1470s a Spanish fleet of two dozen small ships captured the Genoese colony on Santiago and took Antonio da

Noli himself hostage, demanding that Genoa pay a thousand gold doubloons for his ransom. It was Portugal, however, that rescued him and returned him to his plantations. Although the Genoese plantations remained modest, Antonio da Noli's son-in-law nevertheless managed to harvest sufficient cane in 1508 to export 400 tons of sugar on a small fleet of merchant vessels. The crop of the future, however, was to be cotton, and this survived better on the poor soils of the Cape Verdes. Like sugar, it was to become one of the great slave-grown crops of the Atlantic colonies.

The Cape Verde Islands were as near as any land could be to the heart of the Atlantic world. As such they became the focal point for exchanges of food plants and domestic animals that were to transform the modern world. Atlantic islands hitherto colonised were sufficiently temperate to be able to feed their populations on European crops such as wheat and barley. The Cape Verdes, by contrast, were deep in the tropics and the colonisers had to learn about a whole new range of food plants that were suitable for the soils and climates that they were to encounter as they moved south and west through the Atlantic. The main cereal crops of Africa were millet and sorghum, and these could be grown on the dry and fairly sterile Cape Verdes to feed both immigrants and slaves. In wetter conditions the key African crop was rice, and this was later carried across the Atlantic to become the preferred crop in some new colonies in both North and South America. A less familiar crop from tropical Africa that became important for feeding colonial labour gangs was the vegetable banana. When roasted, steamed or fried the banana – or plantain – became a major source of carbohydrate used by immigrant African communities on the Atlantic islands and in the New World. An equally important migration of crops was the one that returned across the Atlantic from the New World. The potato tuber, which spread widely in eighteenth-century Europe, was of little use in tropical colonies, but the cassava root – or manioc – became one of the fundamental sources of food on colonial plantations and in colonial ships, especially those carrying slaves. Even more dramatic in its impact than cassava was the spread of maize, which was gradually adopted as the major food crop throughout much of Africa and on the islands.

The Cape Verdes were a point of exchange and experiment not only in crop farming, but in animal husbandry. Although Africa had long reared sheep and goats as well as hens and cows, such livestock was new not only on the Cape Verdes but more spectacularly on the

American islands and shores to which animals were carried by the first transatlantic colonists. On the Cape Verdes livestock could wander virtually unsupervised and multiply freely before being seized and put on boats. The islands were fortunate in having a plentiful supply of salt with which to preserve butchered meat that could be sold to passing vessels, along with fresh water and vegetables, and they became breeding grounds for not only edible animals but beasts of burden. Donkeys, horses and mules could be reared on tropical islands that were relatively free of the diseases that affected the African mainland. Cape Verde livestock was also cheaper than the animals ferried south on the long voyage from Europe.

The role of the Cape Verdes as a way-station took on a particular new importance in 1500 when the Atlantic sea route to India was opened by Vasco da Gama. The long haul from Goa, in Portuguese India, back to Lisbon was slow and precarious. Many of the heavy East India sailing vessels barely survived the voyage out to India and back once, let alone twice. When needing help they found most of the African coast inaccessible with few deep harbours and no good repair facilities either for their worm-eaten hulls or for their storm-torn sails. The island of Santiago therefore became one of the most welcome landfalls for sailors who had successfully rounded the Cape of Good Hope on their homeward journey in vessels laden with black peppers. By the later sixteenth century the islands also benefited from the opening up of Brazil to colonisation. The Genoese plantations on the Cape Verdes supplied Brazil with its first sugar canes and the Portuguese herdsmen on the islands sent livestock to South America that formed the basis of the Brazilian hide and leather industry. Before Brazil's economy took root, however, another Atlantic island was planted by settlers, creating one more model for the European colonisation of the New World.

The island of São Tomé lies two thousand miles east of the Cape Verdes along the equator. It is some 300 miles south of the Niger delta and 500 miles north of the Congo estuary. Like all the sugar islands except the Canaries, São Tomé had not been inhabited when the first European sailors sighted it in the 1470s, but by the 1490s it had been absorbed into the new colonial world. The island's first lord-proprietor, João de Paiva, failed to make a success of his settlement in the 1480s at a time when the colonial energies of a vigorous Portuguese king, John II, were being devoted to exploring the newly recognised resources of the African mainland. Rather than take direct responsibility for the island, the Portuguese crown issued a revised charter of colonisation to Alvaro de Camina, a member of the royal household. He was granted wide powers and opportunities that he was able to use to good effect. At the same time the heir to the Portuguese throne created a similar charter for the nearby island of Príncipe – the prince's island – and gave it to the Carneiro family. Like the chartered captains of Madeira, a generation earlier, the agents of the new lords-proprietor initially extracted wealth from São Tomé by felling tropical timber and growing food crops. They then devoted their earnings to the planting of sugar-cane.

The sugar planters of São Tomé were neither Castilian nor Genoese but Portuguese. Like other colonial lords-proprietor, however, they had great difficulty in attracting settlers despite the fertility of the soils, the plentiful rain and a year-round growing season in the tropical climate. Some of the early colonists were convicts and orphans sent out against their will. The most successful settlers were apparently recruited among the spasmodically persecuted ethnic minorities of Portugal. Jews, or Jewish migrants who had fled to Portugal from Spain, came to constitute a significant element in the population. Their presence was less hidden than in the Canary Islands and their success in establishing the sugar industry on both São Tomé and Príncipe was acknowledged.

The São Tomé sugar industry was slow to expand and the records of its productivity are incomplete. Although the island had the climatic advantage of being able to grow cane to a full height of six feet in only five months, the humid atmosphere made the curing of sugar loaves more difficult than on the drier islands, and most of São Tomé's sugar was described as 'red' rather than white. When finished the sugar loaves had to be dried in oast-like barns where they were laid on high racks above charcoal embers designed to give off as little smoke as possible so as not to spoil the flavour of the sugar. The scale of production did eventually match that of both Madeira and Tenerife and the careful calculations of Magalhães Godinho suggest that by 1580 the island may have been the Atlantic's largest sugar-producing colony. Fragmentary documents indicate that at its peak the island had, in addition to its horse- and slave-worked mills, no less than seventy large water wheels driving the sugar mills. If each mill averaged a yield of thirty tons of refined sugar, annual exports would have reached 2,000 tons. At the same period some sixty sailing vessels were said to be leaving São Tomé each year. If each of these registered vessels, together with a few that escaped the supervision of the royal tax collectors, could carry thirty tons of sugar, the annual export figure would also have been about 2,000 tons. Some estimates, however, have put São Tomé production as high as 2,800 tons (Magalhães Godinho, 1981: IV, 94–9).

Even more important than the scale of the São Tomé sugar production was its role as the pioneer in developing the concept of the slave plantation. All-black slave gangs became the key to the new Atlantic system of plantations that developed in the seventeenth century in both North and South America. Since São Tomé was unable to attract white working immigrants, such as those who went to Madeira, or recruit local conscripts, like those attached to the estates of the Canaries, the only plantation workers available to the island comprised slave labour bought from the black populations on the surrounding shores of Africa. The scale of the trade in slaves grew dramatically, and in 1516 the island allegedly imported no less than 4,000 slaves, though many of them were intended to be re-exported rather than kept for work on the sugar plantations. Slaves who stayed on the plantations, and survived the harsh conditions, were noted in Europe for the large profits that they generated for their owners. The technology of the Atlantic sugar industry had evolved on the island of Madeira, but the labour model that spread to later colonies was that pioneered on the slave estates of São Tomé. Although the production of São Tomé sugar may have been the largest of any Atlantic island, and the slave mode of production may have been the most profitable, the reliability of the supplies arriving back in Europe left much to be desired. French corsairs not only captured returning sugar vessels as they approached Lisbon or Antwerp in European waters, but sent armed ships out to Africa to raid the plantations. Natural hazards, notably fire in the mills, occasionally curtailed production and led to complaints in the Italian city states that sugar had become unusually expensive. But the most volatile aspect of the São Tomé plantation complex was neither fire nor piracy but the constant risk of rebellion in a colony whose population was predominantly made up of slaves. One rebellion that broke out in 1574 resulted in the firing of the town and another, in 1595, led to a mass escape into the hills. It was the risk of such slave revolts that made São Tomé's wealth so precarious and therefore tempted the sugar barons to move their base of operations elsewhere. By 1615 it was alleged that of the seventy-two largest estates on São Tomé fifty-nine had been abandoned. By then, and despite the potential risk of violence, the São Tomé slave mode of production had taken root in the Americas.

In the 1530s the São Tomé plantation system had been introduced into the Caribbean. Spain bought its first boatloads of black slaves and grafted the São Tomé practice of slave management on to its own sugar economy. Within half a century African slaves were also being used on the sugar plantations of Portuguese America, in north-eastern Brazil. By the 1650s, when the English conquered Spanish Jamaica, they too adopted black slavery as their mode of production. The English also introduced sugar and slavery to the several small Caribbean islands on which they had hitherto experimented unsuccessfully with such crops as cotton, indigo and tobacco, all grown by white immigrants from Europe. By the second half of the seventeenth century the English had adopted the São Tomé model of sugar-growing, with an all-black labour force, on Barbados. The profits of the new Atlantic system were carried to Europe but the costs were shouldered by the peoples of Africa.

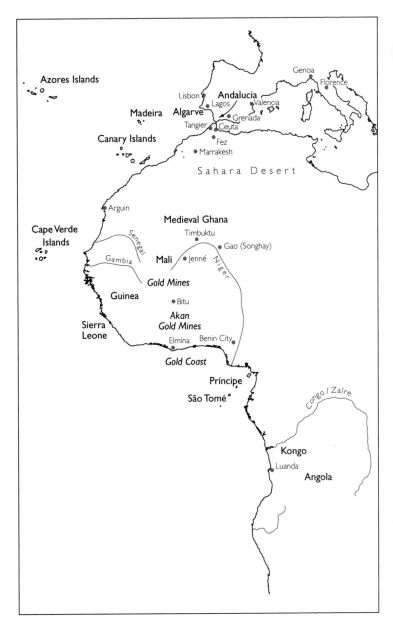

Map 2 Western Africa

CHAPTER TWO

The Merchandise of Africa

While the sea merchants of Europe had been colonising the Atlantic islands, the landed aristocracies were casting covetous eyes on the African mainland. Africa was clearly visible from Europe across the Straits of Gibraltar and the city of Ceuta was well known to the Genoese whose bankers had been buying their gold bullion there for two centuries. Gold was the most famous of all the products of Africa and the one that most attracted successive generations of aspiring colonisers and would-be conquerors. But golden riches were not the only attraction of Africa. Portuguese fishermen from the Algarve regularly sailed small boats across the narrow seas to fish in African waters. In North Africa Morocco was recognised as a fertile agricultural country that had once provided quantities of corn for its Roman colonisers and now supported several flourishing cities at the western end of the Islamic world. On a more sombre note European land-owners who were constantly short of workers to sow and reap their crops could sometimes afford to buy foreigners to work for them as slaves. The traditional, white, slaves of the Mediterranean had been Slav-speaking peoples from the plains of Russia, but the prospect of buying, or even kidnapping, slaves closer to hand in Africa was tempting.

The first conquistadores to set their sights on Africa were Christian knights who had exhausted the opportunities for raiding in the old Muslim lands of southern Europe. For several centuries the frontier between Christendom and Islam had run through the middle of Portugal and Spain, and occasional frontier wars had brought plunder, slaves and conquered farmland to the kingdoms on either side of the border. By the fourteenth century both the Algarve, in southern Portugal, and Andalucia, in southern Spain, had been conquered by the knights of Christendom who had thereby enhanced their own status and wealth. Since then all their efforts to overwhelm Granada, the richest and most resplendent of the Muslim kingdoms of Spain, had been effectively resisted. At the dawn of the fifteenth century the nobility of Europe therefore turned its ambitions towards North Africa. Whereas men in boats had pioneered the colonisation of the Atlantic islands, it was men on horseback who aimed to conquer Morocco. Their ultimate objective was probably to capture the royal city of Fez, nestling at the foot of the Rif Mountains one hundred miles up the road from the Atlantic shore through the plain of Alcacer Kibir. Their first target, however, was the port at Ceuta at the mouth of the Mediterranean.

The capture of Ceuta, the Moroccan city on seven hills, was undertaken by a huge international expedition. The campaign has sometimes been portrayed as the key event that marked the end of the European middle ages and the beginning of a modern era in which Europe emerged from its isolation and began to take a more significant role in world affairs, thereby bringing the dawn of empire. The adventurers who arrived in Africa came from as far away as France and Germany and one English participant financed four of the provision vessels required. Twenty-three other vessels were also commissioned in England. The commander of the expedition, King John I of Portugal, took with him three of his Anglo-Portuguese sons, grandsons of John of Gaunt and cousins of several later kings of England. The fleet assembled at Lagos, on the Algarve coast, on Sunday, 30 July 1415. According to one account, it consisted of 33 galleys, 27 triremes, 32 biremes and 120 smaller vessels commandeered to give assistance. In all the boats allegedly required the services of 30,000 oarsmen and sailors and were able to carry 20,000 soldiers with their weapons, provisions and horses (Major, 1877: 28).

The Ceuta expedition bore some of the hallmarks of the medieval crusades. The objective was largely economic, the capture of land, people and wealth, but the ideological cloak was religious. The enemy was Muslim rather than Christian and therefore the expedition was deemed 'morally' justified, with the commanders of the assault being given the support of the pope in Rome. He granted the invaders the rights that had historically been given to crusaders seeking to recover the 'Holy Land' of Palestine from the so-called 'infidels' of Islam. Once suitably blessed, and assured that at least their God was on their side, the army attempted to make the crossing to Africa. Adverse winds and currents swept some of the largest vessels far beyond their target and into the Mediterranean, but enough small vessels reached the far shore to attack Ceuta, breach the sea defences and capture the walled city. Among those who entered the town was Prince Henry of Portugal, then aged nineteen. He was granted heraldic spurs for his bravery and accorded the chivalric status of a knight by his father. Although Henry crossed over to Ceuta again three years later, when the Spanish kingdom of Granada threatened to recapture the city on behalf of Islam, such ferry trips were apparently the furthest that he ever sailed. Henry was first and foremost a landed nobleman and it was not until the nineteenth century that romantic historians gave him the nickname 'the navigator' for his role in financing the colonial expeditions into Africa.

The success of the Portuguese royal family, and of the Portuguese landed nobility, in creating Europe's first modern colony of immigrant settlers on the African mainland was limited but lasting. Not until 1640 did the Portuguese lose Ceuta to Castile, and only in 1660 did they surrender Tangier, the other great North African harbour that they captured, to England. The economic success of the small foreign settlement on the northern plain of Atlantic Morocco was largely confined to agriculture. At its most extensive the sphere of colonial domination south of Tangier probably never exceeded in scope the size of Madeira and the crop that was most successfully produced was wheat. Unlike the Madeira colonists, the Morocco settlers were able to recruit some local labour to help them with their tilling, reaping and winnowing of cereals. In addition to wheat they planted a significant acreage of barley. Settler relations with their neighbours were not always harmonious, however, and cattle rustling was a profitable activity that frequently put the colony on a war footing. Four great fortresses were built for such emergencies and they protected the settlers and their booty until peace could be restored.

The limited achievements of conquest in northern Morocco were followed by an initially rather more successful policy of commercial dealing along the southern coast of the Moroccan kingdom. The great plains between the city of Marrakesh and the Atlantic were described as a veritable sea of wheat. A second set of four Portuguese fortresses was established along the southern coast to protect the interests of traders. Trade was not always more peaceful than colonisation and on one occasion Portuguese vessels succeeded in capturing the Moroccan wheat fleet to Grenada as it set off to supply the great Muslim cities of southern Spain. Meanwhile, the Algarve continued to trade with Morocco, supplying fruit in exchange for grain. After 1450 the Moroccan wheat trade took on a new importance for Portugal when Madeira abandoned cereal farming and switched its land and labour resources to the growing of sugar, forcing the Portuguese corn merchants to rely increasingly on alternative sources of wheat. At the same time the Portuguese trading posts were visited by ships travelling ever further down the Atlantic coast and requiring supplies both for their crews and for the African trade factories they established beyond the Sahara.

Even in times of peace, trading through the Portuguese fortresses of south Morocco was not always successful. When the harvests were bad the settler towns could not even feed their own garrisons, let alone supply Lisbon, and the colonial commanders had to buy corn urgently from the Azores, or even from Germany. In the early sixteenth century the garrisons were staffed by some 5,000 soldiers but so dire was their condition of life that few would-be immigrants went to Morocco voluntarily. The Moroccan forts gained a reputation for being sinks of depravity filled with convicts who had no compunction about raiding even the most peaceable of neighbouring communities for women, livestock and newly gathered harvests. Such brigandry, however, was scarcely discouraged when Spain and Portugal still offered an open market for slaves, and kidnapping was a more lucrative employment than farming. While male captives were sent to Portugal to till the neglected soils of the southern plain or to harvest sugar on the Portuguese islands, women were viciously taken away by bawdy young princes anxious to satisfy their sadistic fantasies about life in a Moorish harem. Portuguese activity in the unsavoury walled towns of southern Morocco eventually dwindled away, however, while in northern Morocco a much more regular caravan trade in fine textiles and ornate leather goods grew up to link Tangier with the city of Fez through the plain of Alcacer Kibir. This northern trade, and the surviving communities of Portuguese peasants along the route, eventually brought a renewed military interest in Morocco on the part of the Portuguese crown.

The leader of the new Portuguese conquistadores of the 1570s was the young King Sebastian. Like his fifteenth-century predecessors he imagined his military campaign to be a crusade. Its timing, however, suggests a more mercenary origin. By the 1570s Portuguese success in Asia was in decline while a new Portuguese empire in South America had not yet proved its potential. The young king therefore revived his country's ambitions in North Africa and mounted a new attack on Morocco. The venture, however, was doomed. Many of the 16,000 soldiers whom he took with him were ill-trained raw recruits and his artillery was inadequate for a modern campaign. Worse still, the Portuguese cavalry was no match for their Berber counterparts of the Moroccan empire. Not only was the invading army spectacularly defeated halfway down the road from Tangier to Fez, but the rash young king vanished in the rout. For many years mourning Portuguese patriots expected him to be ransomed and brought home to restore their national pride. He never was, though the myth of his survival, or even resurrection, was still vibrant in the 1640s. The defeat of Sebastian on the plain of Alcacer Kibir heralded the temporary eclipse of Portugal's independence and the country was soon seized by the Spanish Habsburgs. In the meantime, however, both royal and merchant Portuguese interest had been largely diverted away from North Africa and towards West Africa thanks to the opening of the tropical sea-lanes in the Atlantic.

European progress in exploring the farther reaches of the African mainland went hand in hand with the exploitation of the adjacent islands. Until the 1430s sailors were reluctant to pass much beyond the latitude of the Canaries for fear that the southward currents would sweep them into an unknown torrid zone from which there would be no return. Improved triangular sails, which enabled their small boats to tack across the winds and therefore make progress against the prevailing current, encouraged the hardy to explore further south, and by the 1440s they had travelled beyond the Saharan desert latitudes and were exploring the shore opposite the Cape Verdes. It was there that new slave raids were attempted, but seizing 'Moorish' and then 'Negro' captives was not the only lure. The Italian chroniclers also began to report small finds of gold along the coast. Caravans using the little-frequented western tracks across the desert carried at least some gold dust among the commodities with which they returned to Morocco. Provided they were not frightened off by threats of kidnapping, these caravans were sometimes willing to trade a little gold for some of the ships' stores that the explorers carried on their ventures. One Atlantic inlet along the Saharan coast, south of Tenerife, was optimistically even named the river of gold, the Spanish Rio de Oro. A more promising trading site was found by the Portuguese, who reached the island of Arguin, in Mauritania, and built a small commercial fortress there in 1448. The little Portuguese fort at Arguin became the first European trade castle in tropical Africa, and over the next centuries was regularly captured, lost and recaptured by the French, the English and the Dutch.

In 1447, the year before the walled trading factory was built on Arguin Island, a systematic report on the gold trade of Africa was drafted in Italy. Antonio Malfante, of the Genoese banking house of Centurione, garnered his intelligence at the oasis of Tuat, 500 miles north of Timbuktu. His informant, whose brother was a commercial agent in Timbuktu, boasted that he had been a resident in that city for thirty years and had built up a personal fortune of 16,000 ounces of gold while trading deep into the 'land of the blacks'. He claimed, improbably, that in West Africa silver was so scarce that it fetched its weight in gold. In North Africa, which traditionally bought most of its silver from Europe, the ratio had normally been more akin to five ounces of silver to one ounce of gold. The trade was so lucrative that one medieval estimate claimed that the Muslim world imported as much as forty tons of silver a year from the mines of Germany and the Balkans and paid in return eight tons of African gold each year. Even if the estimates were seriously exaggerated it was hardly surprising that Europeans were so keen to find the source of the gold and to open their own direct maritime access to the mines.

A more significant opening into this flourishing commercial world of Africa than the Mauritania castle of Arguin proved to be the Gambia River. It was here that hit-and-run raids began to give way to more systematic attempts to establish long-term diplomatic and economic ties with Africa's peoples. Traders from Europe – Italian, French, Castilian and Catalan as well as Portuguese – tried to win the goodwill of any coastal trading kingdom that could provide them with economic intelligence about the structure of the long-distance trade in gold. Ideally they hoped to find brokers who could help them draw some of the trade towards the coast. Between 1440 and 1460 all the Guinea creeks, harbours and beaches between the hidden mouth of the Senegal River and the open harbour of Sierra Leone were explored. The exotic commodities that the seafaring foreigners offered, and the prices at which they made them available, always had to be competitive with those of the local wholesalers who had previously been supplied overland from Morocco.

The history of Atlantic colonisation in the rivers of Guinea was wholly different from the history of colonial enterprise in Morocco in the fifteenth and sixteenth centuries. In Morocco the Portuguese tried, with an admittedly limited degree of success, to establish communities of settlers and traders protected by colonial garrisons. In Guinea, by contrast, the Portuguese decided to discourage white traders from settling on the coast and refused to contemplate the expense of building commercial castles or of establishing regular military control over the miles of open trading beaches. There is little evidence to suggest that the Portuguese were particularly successful in tapping the Moroccan end of the African gold trade. In Guinea, by contrast, significant if unmeasured quantities of gold do seem to have been diverted from the old Saharan trading system to the new Atlantic one. The gold dust that was offered to sea merchants on the Gambia River and along the Guinea coast came from two different sets of gold mines, Bambuk on the upper Senegal and Bouré on the upper Niger, each about 300 miles inland. These mines had flourished for centuries and were major sources of supply for both Europe and the Mediterranean throughout the middle ages. Both the gold dust and the more spectacular gold nuggets were commended by eleventh-century Muslim chroniclers who received glowing reports of the great gold market of Ghana, on the southern fringe of the Sahara, although it seems a little improbable that the king of Ghana should actually have tethered his horse to a giant nugget of gold as was reported. The trans-Saharan trade had attracted a large community of merchants to the city of Ghana where they established their Muslim ghetto a few miles from the king's palace and away from the sacred groves of his ancestral shrines. The merchants were attended by innkeepers, interpreters, moneylenders, camel-breeders, insurance agents, accountants and by the holy guardians of the different mosques that catered for the needs of Muslim visitors of varied ethnic origin. By the time the Portuguese reached the coast of West Africa, however, this old desert-side market and its royal twin city had vanished into the sands and the main international emporium had been relocated to Timbuktu on the middle bend of the Niger River. The new riverside kingdom of Mali dominated the southern Saharan markets and monitored the business activities of the autonomous chiefdoms that controlled the gold-bearing gravel-pits of Bambuk and Bouré. By the fourteenth century the Mali kings had adopted Islam as their own religion and the royal cities had tall mosques of clay bricks thronged with local black worshippers, to the amazement of white visitors who crossed the desert from Spain, Sicily and Morocco.

The Mali empire was the desired destination for the first generation of seaborne traders to West Africa. Tapping into the thriving international land trade from a remote and previously ignored coast presented an immense challenge to the sea traders, yet dozens of small trading vessels began to skirt the Saharan shores in the hope of finding golden wealth. Some were successful. From the 1460s through to the 1680s the primary export from the many small trading beaches around the westernmost shore of West Africa was gold from the inland rivers rather than ivory or slaves or the agricultural produce of coastal farms. Gold was the most important single item of sea trade, but the Europeans probably never succeeded in creating an ocean link capable of effectively rivalling the well-established desert link to Morocco. Ships may have travelled a little faster than caravans, and they kept going during the night while camels had to sleep, but overall boats were not much more reliable, or cost-effective, than beasts. When a lone Portuguese 'embassy' did finally succeed in penetrating the deep interior of West Africa, and reaching the royal capital of Mali, the king was amazed to hear that Europe had cities that compared in magnificence with Baghdad, but he showed no inclination to switch his international trade dealings from the world of Islam to that of Christendom, or from the desert to the ocean.

One of the striking features of early Atlantic history is this almost complete failure of Europeans to penetrate or conquer any of the West African kingdoms. Instead, the Portuguese and their associates and rivals steadily built up a string of trading beaches along the whole Guinea coast. The system was small in scale and informal in structure, each trading initiative had to test the commercial climate and use local contacts to explore the range of commodities most in demand. One prestigious item of trade that Europeans were able to bring by ship was horses, which did not breed well in the African tropics. The overland supply from Morocco was also rather limited and while some caravaneers invested in expensive bloodstock that they led by camel across the desert, the venture was a hazardous gamble. On the alternative sea route the horses disliked the roll and pitch of small boats but many nevertheless survived the voyage to give the sea traders a very specific commercial entrée into West Africa. The status of West African kings was commensurate with the quality of their steeds and they greatly appreciated the 'Barbary' horses that the Portuguese could ferry round the coast from Morocco. On feast days and religious festivals kings rode out on richly caparisoned mounts, for each of which they might be willing to pay as much as seven human slaves. The bargain was even more glittering when the kings were willing to include a little gold dust in the price.

A dominant element in the traditional African trade in gold was the international trade in salt. This trade was very familiar to European mariners who took thousands of tons of salt each year from southern Europe to northern Europe. An equally important and well-established pattern of salt trading was the one that brought rock salt from the great quarries of the Sahara to the cities of West Africa. Slabs of salt were dug from the beds of dried salt lakes by gangs of slaves and loaded on to the backs of camels. Such was the scarcity of salt throughout the interior of West Africa that many communities, including large urban ones, were willing to pay for it with gold. The salt was not only consumed immediately as a food condiment, but became a local retail currency that the towns could use to buy food from the countryside or craft wares from village potters and black-smiths. The long-distance trade in salt depended, however, on high-quality rock-like salt that was easy to transport and did not dissolve too readily when the weather turned humid. The sea merchants had no difficulty in finding lagoon salt along the coast, and more especially in the salt pans on the Cape Verde Islands, but they did not have the qual-ity of supply, or the means of overland transport, to compete with the great salt merchants of the Sahara. The Europeans turned instead to trading in that other essential, but heavy, raw material on which mod-ern agrarian economies depended: iron.

The African iron trade created a new form of exchange currency based on the standardised weight of an iron bar. Although most com-munities had their own supply of iron-ore, and the wooded coast of West Africa did not lack charcoal for smelting, the local ironmasters did not provide enough high-quality wrought iron to satisfy demand in all the village smithies. European bars of wrought iron therefore sold well among local blacksmiths who supplied their farming cus-tomers with axes, hoes, machetes and adzes. They also sold the war-lords the necessary lances, arrowheads, bayonets and spears with which to conduct military policy. For the Portuguese, investing in large quantities of acceptable wrought iron that could be sold in West Africa for small payments in gold dust presented problems since Portugal itself was short of good iron and so had to buy its stocks of iron bars from expensive specialist suppliers such as the Basques of northern Spain. Despite the high costs, the iron trade succeeded to the point where historians have asked whether the impact of Atlantic trading on Africa was so intense that it undermined local metal industries and created a type of artificially induced dependency. Any thesis of such 'underdevelopment' needs to be studied carefully, however, since the people of Guinea never became wholly dependent on foreign supplies of iron but could always maintain some bargaining strength by contrasting the value of imported iron bars with that of locally forged ones. Only when the price was right, and the means of payment were available, did the hard-headed African men of business close their deals. They made their economic choices rationally and were not as gullible as the sea traders had hoped they might be.

Even more important trading commodities than iron in the economy of the Guinea rivers were textiles. It was in the trading of cotton cloth that the Portuguese made their greatest commercial breakthrough. Portugal itself did not have a thriving textile industry and the merchants from Lisbon and the Algarve could not afford to buy many bolts of expensive English or Flemish woollen cloth that would compete with the local West African cotton materials. Instead, the Portuguese sponsored a cotton industry on the Cape Verde Islands, a mere ferry ride from the Guinea coast. Slave craftsmen were brought to the islands where they introduced African-style looms and wove traditional cotton strips that could then be sewn together to make cloth of any width. Plantations of indigo were established next to the Cape Verde cotton fields and supplied dyeing vats in which the cotton strips were turned into blue material. The blue-and-white island cloaks matched the traditional quality of African textiles and provided the Portuguese with a commodity that satisfied the demands of customers willing to purchase cloth in exchange for gold.

The gold-trading beaches of Guinea stretched as far south as the great natural harbour of Sierra Leone. Beyond that the tropical forest was almost uninhabited and the colonial adventurers of the Portuguese royal family temporarily stopped investing in new African exploration. Instead they rented out the right to exploit West Africa's forest resources to a private merchant named Fernão Gomes. It was he who made the next gold strike in Africa. In 1471 reports began to trickle back to Lisbon, Dieppe, Venice and elsewhere that 700 miles beyond Sierra Leone gold could be bought at a creekside village inhabited by the Akan-speaking people of the forest. The ethnic term Akan became synonymous, in European eyes, with a specialised gold trader and the Akan coast was later named the Gold Coast. The creekside village was christened 'the village of the mine', Elmina, and within ten years a trading fortress had been built beside it, similar to the one built thirty-five years earlier to store gold and commercial wares on the Saharan coast at Arguin. The sea merchants at Elmina thought that they had at last found a viable gateway to the mining territories of the far interior. In fact they had discovered a harbour that served an entirely new mining complex, one that had been opened less than a hundred years earlier.

In the late middle ages the worldwide search for gold had been revived when international trade expanded again after the acute recession that had accompanied the Black Death and the halving of the Old World's population. The inland mines of Bambuk and Bouré had been unable to respond to new incentives to produce more gold since their mineral reserves were low, and late fourteenth-century gold prospectors roamed ever further south until they struck new deposits in the forest. A highway for porters and donkeys was opened linking a river port on the Niger at Jenné to a trading town on the northern edge of the forest at Bitu. A farmer's quarter for the local people, an industrial quarter for the ironsmiths, a Muslim quarter for the merchants and a market where foreign textiles could be stored in safety to await the Akan-speaking miners who brought gold dust out of the forest were all built at Bitu. One of the commercial specialities that had been important in opening the forest trade had been the trade in copper and brass, easily worked metals that were not naturally available to the Akan. Items known to have been sold at Bitu included ornate brass platters and copper ewers fashioned by the Muslim craftsmen of the Mediterranean, metal bowls decorated in Syria and oil lamps of the style used by Christian Copts in Egypt. Gold was cautiously offered in exchange for such treasures but the Akan took astute care to avoid being captured or tricked by business opponents. Such was the mistrust that forest dwellers showed towards the grassland traders, and so great was the safe distance they adopted, that witnesses to the trade described it as a 'dumb barter' in which little face-to-face bargaining took place and deals were brokered at arm's length. It was this dumb trade at Bitu that the Portuguese heard about after they landed at Elmina in 1471.

The scale of Akan gold production is difficult to estimate but reasoned guesses suggest that each year it may have run to a ton of pure metal, perhaps 30,000 ounces. Salt and textiles were the main form of payment, along with occasional fine objects. In addition to trade wares the earliest Akan miners probably imported grassland slaves to clear the forest, dig pits in which to seek gold ore and plant food crops for the growing mine population. The mining industry was always dangerous and free men preferred to use lowly foreign slaves to perform the most risky tasks. The mines were frequently engulfed by mud slides that suffocated the men, women and children who had been sent down to work them. Any gold ore that was hauled to the surface had to be painstakingly crushed with heavy pestles pounding the rock in great mortars. Crushed ore, together with gold-bearing sands dredged out of the streams, had then to be washed to reveal the tiny flecks of gold. Standing all day in cold water was almost as punishing an occupation as being lowered down an unventilated mine shaft. Both tasks were probably undertaken by slaves, though under the closest supervision to counteract theft and smuggling.

Once the gold had been extracted from the forest pits, and sold to the traders who visited Bitu, it had to be carried north, packed in heavy money belts, by traders accompanied by armed guards. At the river port of Jenné the traders boarded the huge river canoes in which teams of paddlers had each brought a ton of rock salt upstream. The gold carriers were then escorted downstream to Timbuktu accompanied by archers equipped to repel river pirates keen to capture the new booty coming out of the forest. Soon after 1471, when the Atlantic sailors had first learnt of the existence of this trading complex, the key stretch of inland waterway between Jenné and Timbuktu fell under the political and military domination of new African masters from Songhay. The Songhay empire, which was rooted in the 500-year-old river port downstream from Timbuktu, had recently emerged as a great naval power on the upper Niger. Its armed canoes began to control and tax all the international traffic on the river and Songhay became an even more formidable obstacle to European aspirations in Africa than the now fragmented empire of Mali. The Portuguese could not attempt a military challenge to an inland trading empire and so competition between Songhay and Portugal for the gold of the forest was undertaken by commercial means. The Atlantic creek at Elmina, only 100 miles south of the forest gold pits, had a potential commercial advantage over the Songhay river port at Jenné, 300 miles north of the forest. Exploiting the logistical opportunity, and winning a significant share of the Akan gold shipments, nevertheless took patience and enterprise on the part of the Atlantic adventurers.

Initially the Portuguese at Elmina found it difficult to compete with Muslim rivals. The craftsmanship of their brass wares did not match the artistic refinement of the competing objects on offer, though sea transport did efficiently supply large quantities of basic copper and brass that Akan craftsmen would later melt down as raw material. Heavy copper bracelets and brass shaving basins were accepted less for their functional use and more for the value of scarce metal that could be refashioned as ornaments that satisfied local aesthetic requirements. For some decorative purposes copper was more useful than gold and Pacheco Pereira, when governor of the trading castle at Elmina, reported that copper and brass, like spices, saffron and sugar, were items of which Portugal should always have a plentiful supply. A much more important part of the trade, however, was the very sensitive market in textiles. Pacheco Pereira also reported that red and blue cloth had been so valuable in Jenné that it was sold by the yard rather than by the roll. High-class African merchants particularly appreciated silk, which came across the desert from Spain, but Portugal produced no silk and its traders could not afford to bring foreign silks to Africa. The textiles in which the Portuguese sea merchants did invest were cottons, woollens and linens. The fashions in greatest demand were Muslim and the Portuguese found that they had to purchase long gowns with hoods in Morocco to ensure that they were of a style and quality recognised by the very selective Akan wholesalers. Shippers could not risk having cloth of unacceptable quality being rejected and returned the 3,000 miles to Lisbon. Fashion-conscious customers, some of them the minor nobility of the Akan chiefdoms, liked the styles fashioned by tailors in the inland cities of West Africa. They could not immediately be seduced into buying the unfamiliar ready-to-wear garments supplied by the trading castle at Elmina.

One of the great problems of maintaining a large warehouse in the humid tropics was that the bales of textiles and racks of clothing were constantly liable to become damp and stained with mildew. The factors also complained that customers sorting through the materials for the most attractive colours, and clambering over the bales seeking the best qualities, damaged and dirtied their stock. Locally made cotton strips were the most common item of trade, while the more valuable coloured materials came from Europe. Many of the coloured cloths were not used as pieces but were unravelled for their thread and rewoven according to the intricate *kente* tartans favoured by eminent Africans. Among the finest pieces imported were cotton prints that the

Portuguese had brought round the Cape of Good Hope from India and sold to Africa when they could find no other way to beat the competition from their Muslim rivals. The Portuguese crown, which claimed a monopoly on all branches of the gold and textile trade, tried to prevent any private deals or unauthorised bargaining and insisted that any soiled or substandard materials must be shipped back to Lisbon rather than sold at a discount. The large bales of second-hand clothing that formed one part of the trade were carefully inspected to ensure that torn or faulty shirts, gowns and suits would be returned to the supplier in Europe at the invoiced price rather than informally bartered for gold in Africa.

Although textiles formed the most important item of trade in all the early Atlantic empires, cloth alone was not sufficiently valuable to enable Europeans to capture a major share of the Akan gold trade. As early as 1479 the Flemish trader Eustache de la Fosse discovered that his best hope of buying gold was to stock his ship with slaves on his way down the Guinea coast and then sell the slaves again when he arrived on the Gold Coast. The Portuguese soon adopted a similar policy, ignoring the inconvenient fact that slaves who had been bought by Christians, and who had been promised baptism and spiritual salvation, were in fact being resold to mine-owners who worshipped their own quite different deities. Many of the slaves sold to the mines by the Portuguese came not from the Guinea coast but from São Tomé. The island sent a small boatload of captives across to Elmina about every six weeks and at the height of the trade the Akan were probably buying as many as 1,000 slaves each year.

Great excitement was experienced in Elmina Castle every time a foot-caravan of goldsmiths came down to the coast. The traders were ushered into the castle with pomp and fanfare to avoid any suspicion of illicit secret smuggling for which the penalty imposed by the Portuguese captain was the severing of both ears. Once inside the castle the weighing of gold involved a complex ritual in which each protagonist hoped to steal a march on his opponent. The Akan used sets of weights of which they alone knew the value and that enabled them to judge very finely the balance of advantage or disadvantage in each individual bargain. The weights were based on a well-established scale measured in tropical seeds and were cast in brass to form symbols, animals or people. The Portuguese weights, based on the value of the barley grain, were cast, assayed and stamped in the customs house in Lisbon. The factor at Elmina possessed over 200 stamped weights and a fine pair of scales made of silver. When bought, each lot of gold dust was poured through a hole in the trading counter into a leather-lined chest locked with three separate keys. On a good day the factor expected to outwit his suppliers by making a bonus of 20 per cent on the weighings. As soon as the dealers had left the castle the three key-holders were summoned to open the chest in the presence of the castle captain and reweigh the gold accurately so that the bargaining increment could be recorded in the record book. Meanwhile, the Akan merchants, equally satisfied with the bargains they had driven, returned to the forest with their columns of porters carrying bales of textiles, chests of costumes, crates of brass kettles and baskets of beads.

Elmina might be described as the first European 'colony' in tropical Africa. It served the dual role of a fortified warehouse, sufficiently well stocked to attract the Akan goldsmiths, and a military castle, sufficiently well fortified to drive away European 'interlopers' whose ships had not been 'licensed' to trade in West Africa by the Portuguese royal bureaucracy. Fifty years after its foundation the fortress-city boasted fifty-six expatriate citizens and was ruled by a powerful royal captain with a salary of 800 milreis, ten personal attendants and judicial powers to try and sentence not only those who lived in the castle but the client peoples of the African township. The survival of this micro-colony in a zone of endemic malaria, and under constant fear of ship-borne plague, was partially facilitated by a surgeon, a barber who could undertake bloodletting, a male nurse and a pharmacist who dispensed Portuguese medicines and consulted African herbalists. Defence was the responsibility of two artillery officers who kept the heavy guns in working order, but each citizen was expected to provide his own breastplate, helmet, sword and lance and to be able to operate crossbows and matchlocks that were issued by the captain when the castle was besieged. The spiritual needs of the colony were catered for by the castle vicar, assisted by three chaplains and a choir of African children. A master baker employed four Portuguese women to make European-style bread for the garrison's rations, but the superintendent of provisions employed black slave women for all the minor domestic chores. Provisioning the castle was always difficult since the royal supervisors feared that any trade with local suppliers was liable to present opportunities for smuggling and for illicit gold buying. Some of the castle's meat was bought not from local Akan butchers but from colonial suppliers of livestock based on São Tomé.

In the middle of the sixteenth century the success of Elmina as a trading colony began to have repercussions in the interior. The small principalities that grew up behind the Elmina coast, and adopted the commercial ideas and political titles of the old empire of Mali, so facilitated the southward passage of caravans that the share of the gold travelling north dwindled to the point of causing alarm in Songhay. An army of horsemen was sent down from the Niger to revitalise the northward flow of gold but the armed adventure failed. As the surrender of the gold trade to the Atlantic merchants accelerated, the reverberations reached north across the desert. The sultan of Morocco, after his country's success in battle against the Portuguese at Alcacer Kibir in 1578, decided to recover the lost trading initiative in West Africa by force. His bold venture succeeded at a military level when in 1591 a Moroccan cavalry force, supported by a hired regiment of Spanish musketeers, crossed the Sahara and captured Timbuktu. In economic and commercial terms, however, the victory was limited and the pasha appointed as viceroy of Timbuktu was not able significantly to stem the flow of gold towards the Atlantic. Within ten years of the Moroccan campaign a dynamic new European nation had sent ocean traders from Holland to the Gold Coast and some of the gold that had once reached Timbuktu was henceforth shipped to Amsterdam.

Gold had been the obsessive lure that drew Europeans to Africa but where no gold was available merchants tried to make a profit out of slaves. Prince Henry's first forays down the Atlantic coast had been conducted in search of gold, but the profits of his enterprise were based first and foremost on slaving. Protests against the activities of early slaving agents had led to remonstrations by popes who wanted to convert rather than capture the people of Africa. Moral revulsion against the slave trade was largely ineffectual and the role of the Church in trying to protect the natural rights of indigenous peoples was restricted by the power of those who made profits. When Henry the Navigator died in 1460 the slave trade to Europe continued to grow under the auspices of Prince Ferdinand, his adopted nephew, and later of the Portuguese crown which took over responsibility for the Atlantic ventures. When no gold was found on the African coast beyond Elmina traders redoubled their efforts to buy slaves.

Five hundred miles to the east of Elmina, opposite the sugar island of São Tomé, the traders found five navigable creeks that they nicknamed the slave rivers. Fifty miles inland from the coast, beyond a wilderness of swamps, they also discovered the great city of Benin and a kingdom that stretched far into the forests of the lower Niger. Kingdoms were relatively unfamiliar to Africa's explorers and they approached Benin with some awe. The royal palace was immense and its dozens of walled courtyards housed the courtiers who ran the government, the priests who attended the shrines and the king's ceremonial wives. The king himself was normally secluded within the palace and only came out in public on the most awesome of the year's high days and holidays. The maze of palace buildings was so intricate that the Spanish friars who visited Benin in the seventeenth century had great difficulty in finding their way around the complex and in contacting any of the diplomatic officers whom they wished to meet. The Dutch estimated that the city was large even when compared to the towns of the Netherlands and the miles of ruined fortifications can still be traced on the ground.

The splendour of Benin was based on not only its extensive architecture but its fine arts. For at least a thousand years the tradition of clay modelling had produced striking figurines of terracotta that survive in the artistic record long after even the finest wooden carvings have decayed. In Benin the art of metal casting, with wax moulds and molten bronze, gave an even finer and more permanent finish to the beautifully reproduced replicas of royal heads. Artists also made brass plaques depicting scenes of court and city life. After 1480 the scenes began to include bas-relief images of Europeans carrying their fearsome firearms. While the clay-modelling artists moved to brass casting, wood carvers learnt to use ivory as their more durable, valuable and beautiful material. The Portuguese were particularly astonished at the way in which the ivory artists were able to make fine carvings of the foreign sailing ships and Christian religious images, including the Virgin Mary. Ivory, and ivory carvings, provided a supplement to trade in a region with no gold supply.

The first European visitors to Benin were so struck by the symbolism of the royal office that they felt sure Benin must be in contact with the ancient Christian world of Ethiopia in East Africa. One of the Florentine merchants who traded with Benin in 1486 was so convinced of the proximity of the two African empires that he provided the necessary finance to explore the far end of a possible transcontinental trade route and in 1487 a Portuguese diplomatic mission led by Pero de Covilham travelled overland to Ethiopia via Egypt. In the following year, amid renewed excitement at the prospect of finding a Christian route to Asia, the Portuguese crown sponsored Bartholomew Dias to make a fresh exploratory voyage down the Atlantic coast. Although Dias reached the Cape of Good Hope, he failed to find the sea route to Ethiopia and exploration in the remote Atlantic was once again abandoned, and this time was in abeyance for ten years. Instead of looking for the south-west passage to Asia the Portuguese concentrated on investigating the economic resources of Benin itself.

Benin did not show any evidence of a mining industry but its agriculture was extensive. One of the tropical crops that the Portuguese discovered was pepper. Before the opening of the ocean route to India, and the importation of several shiploads of black Asian peppers each year, West Africa's pepper significantly enhanced the grocery trade at Lisbon. In the 1480s colonial merchants discovered that Benin pepper fetched a high price on the spice market in Flanders and in one year Antwerp bought seventy-five hundredweight of Benin peppers. The supply was carefully controlled by the king of Benin who insisted on payment in brass, glass, coral and fine red cloth. His pepper was harvested, dried and compressed into bales complete with the stalks. European buyers were warned to check how much of each bale consisted of stalks when bargaining over prices. Once purchased the bales were carried to the Benin city harbour which small caravels could reach by sailing up thirty miles of inland waterway. The inland trade factory was efficiently supervised by the Benin authorities but from the point of view of foreigners its location was poor since tropical disease was rampant. The European factors in charge of the trade were strongly advised only to visit Benin during the dry season, when malarial mosquitoes were in abeyance. They were also recommended never to drink the local water but to rely instead on wholesome cider from the ships' stores. This admirable advice was not always followed and Benin became a byword for premature death among white traders. Pepper nevertheless continued to attract Portuguese, English and Dutch traders. In the absence of Benin gold the Portuguese offered to buy Benin slaves whom they could resell to the Akan miners on the Gold Coast. For twenty years, from 1487 to 1507, they spasmodically maintained a resident factor in the creekside harbour and Pacheco Pereira regularly visited Benin during his career as Portugal's colonial governor in West Africa. In 1487 the trade in Benin slaves was contracted out to the Florentine merchant Marchione for a fee of 1,100 milreis a year. King Manuel of Portugal tried to stimulate trade relations by sending the Benin king an Arab steed, some Asian silk and jewellery made of European silver. Initially Benin encouraged trade, including trade in convicts and prisoners of war, and sent slaves as gifts to Manuel's European trading partners. In the late 1490s the king sent five slaves to the governor of Elmina and, after Jewish settlers had opened up sugar plantations on São Tomé, he sent their governor gifts of slaves to encourage commercial relations. Some Benin slaves were sent as far as Lisbon, but the key to success for the Portuguese was the selling of carefully selected mine slaves to the Gold Coast at a profit of 500 per cent.

After a start that was auspicious for the dealers, though not for the victims, the Benin slave trade failed to flourish as the Portuguese had anticipated. Although the price of slaves rose with growing demand, and buyers were willing to pay fifty copper manillas for strong men, the king of Benin decided to limit the sale of humans to young women, for whom he accepted 6,000 Indian Ocean cowries apiece, and to keep young men for his own military requirements. Slave buyers might have persuaded the king to change his restrictive policy had they been willing to sell firearms, but selling guns to 'heathens' was deemed to involve unacceptable political risks. Rulers who had been accepted into the Christian community of nations might be permitted to buy matchlocks and the essential supplies of gunpowder to go with them, but in Benin the priests had refused to contemplate any conversion to Christianity. The religious traditionalists even compelled the king to return to the missionaries a fine clock that they had presented to him. The slave trade at Benin therefore dwindled to only 200 slaves a year and in 1507 the trading factory was abandoned. The Portuguese turned for slaves to a new source of supply in the kingdom of Kongo.

This kingdom, a thousand miles south of Benin, had a territory similar in size to Portugal though it was rather more thinly peopled. The ruler was supported by a hierarchy of princes and noblemen who received their political and religious legitimacy from the king in exchange for material offerings of textiles, minerals, currency-shells and food supplies from the provinces. When the king made contact with the first European caravels to call on his coastal estates he rapidly realised that the white aliens might be able to enhance his spiritual authority at the head of the belief system of Kongo. He also thought they might strengthen his political prestige by widening the range of exotic and material possessions that he displayed at his court or gave as rewards to his allies. In 1488 Kongo sent some promising young men to Lisbon to be trained for the priesthood by the Blue Friars of the Order of St John the Evangelist. To gain the greatest benefit from his new Christian allies King Nzinga Nkuwu of Kongo even agreed to go through the required ritual of baptism and himself become a Christian convert. In this the policy of the king was initially quite contrary to that of the king of Benin, who had recognised that religious authority was a key component of political power and that both could be jeopardised by fundamental change.

The king of Kongo soon discovered that any strict adherence to the precepts of Christianity weakened rather than strengthened his traditional sources of power and prestige, as the advisers to the king of Benin had suspected that it might. One way in which kings normally controlled their provinces was by marrying the daughters of governors who were then kept at court. These princesses were held ransom in gilded cages so long as their home provinces remained loyal and paid their taxes. Once the king who had married them became Catholic he discovered that he would be expected to have only one wife and that his status and authority would therefore be seriously diminished. The loss of influence brought about by formal Christian monogamy was accentuated when the king found that his responsibilities for ministering to the needs of his deceased ancestors, and for pouring appropriate libations on the royal graves, were deemed by white priests to be wickedly heathen. The ceremonial taking of bread and wine that symbolised the flesh and the blood of the foreigners' Christ was declared to be incompatible with the traditional Kongo respect for the royal shrines. For sound religious and political reasons the king of Kongo therefore soon found it necessary to rescind his baptismal commitment.

The failure of the first conversion of a king in Kongo did not end the bold Portuguese experiment in Christianisation. To some members of the Kongo élite the commercial and diplomatic attractions of becoming integrated into the new Atlantic community outweighed any spiritual disadvantages. In 1506 a civil war broke out in the kingdom and one of the claimants to the throne threw in his lot with the Christians. Foreign religious backing won him a famous victory for which he gave thanks to St James. The new king took the baptismal name of Afonso and his son took the name of Henry in honour of members of the Portuguese royal family. Henry was appointed to serve the interests of the new faith and sent to Lisbon to train for the priesthood. His studies were successful and before returning to Africa he was elevated to the rank of bishop. His title, however, was that of bishop of Utica, a vacant see in Muslim Algeria, and not bishop of

Kongo. The priests in the Kongo Church remained firmly under Portuguese ecclesiastical patronage and the responsible bishop was the bishop of São Tomé who was himself answerable to the archbishop of Madeira. Bishop Henry died without making his mark on the religious history of his kingdom. His father, however, reigned for forty years and maintained close, though often strained, relations with his fellow Christian kings in Portugal.

Throughout the reign of King Afonso the Kongo Church was in a state of crisis. As early as 1512 a lavish embassy arrived from Portugal to celebrate the close relations of the two kingdoms but it brought controversy. The ambassador was most especially instructed to seek payment for all the gifts and services that Portugal claimed to have showered on Kongo. Since the kingdom produced only a very little ivory and copper, and since the basic industries of iron-smelting, salt-quarrying and textile-weaving did not supply produce of an internationally marketable quality, Kongo was hard pressed when required to settle its balance of payments debts. The Portuguese would naturally have liked settlement in precious metals but none were available and the only form of payment that the white emissaries would accept was slaves. The distressed king therefore sent a convoy of 400 slaves down to the coast so that the ambassador might take his pick of the best of them. No less than 300 were taken and shipped away to the São Tomé slave market. Thereafter relations between Kongo and Portugal were permanently based on ever more pressing demands for slaves. Every priest, monk, friar and scribe who came to work in the Kongo Church expected to be paid in slaves. Even the stonemasons and carpenters sent out to Africa to build the Kongo royal chapel earned their bonuses by trafficking in people. The king complained ever more bitterly about the inhuman grasping of the white courtiers who surrounded him, but he was caught in a mesh from which there was no escape. Kongo, unlike Benin, became a key supplier of slaves to the island plantations of the Atlantic, to the cities of Portugal and Spain, and to the new colonies that were about to be conquered in the Americas.

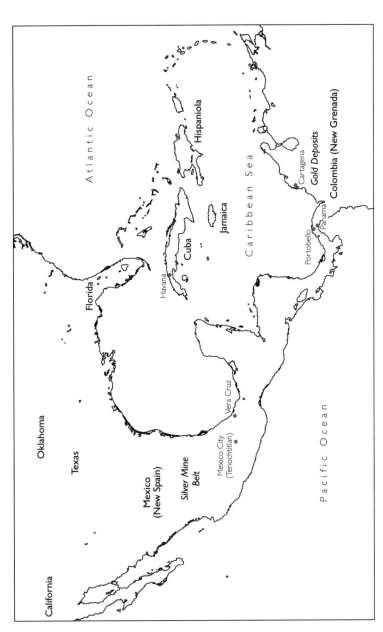

Map 3 The Caribbean

CHAPTER THREE

Spain and the Ocean Crossing

One of the popular questions about the first transatlantic sailing voyage was how much did the venture owe to innovations in science and technology? In 1492 Christopher Columbus, who captained the first voyage, was a fairly experienced if somewhat eccentric mariner. He was forty-one years old and had probably been at sea since his teens. He was also gradually becoming a man of some scholarship and by the time he died in 1506 he had accumulated an impressive library of scientific books that he had annotated with his own observations. His practical knowledge of navigation was usually sound, though he got his winds and his currents slightly wrong when trying to return quickly from his second New World voyage. His cosmographical theory was rather more shaky than his seafaring experience. No serious geographer or astronomer of the late fifteenth century would have denied that the world was round, or that it was therefore theoretically possible to reach China by a western route as well as by the old land route that had taken Venetian traders eastward through the Asian steppes. Any competent mathematician would have known, however, that the circumference of the equator was in the region of 25,000 miles and not the rather smaller figure upon which Columbus optimistically, not to say stubbornly, built his dreams. Columbus thus encountered the Caribbean islands, thirty-three days westward from the Canaries, not so much because he was a better navigator than any rival, but because he was a worse astronomer. When he arrived on the far side of the Atlantic he probably genuinely believed that he had reached islands off the shore of China.

Navigation in the Atlantic Ocean presented real problems for merchants when compared with navigation in the Sahara Desert. Camel caravans, which had been crossing the desert for the last half-millennium, enjoyed the benefit of clear skies and a level horizon against which to measure the altitude of the stars and calculate their progress southward. In the Atlantic, by contrast, the deck of a ship was forever rolling and the sky was frequently overcast. Measurement was often difficult and sailors became accustomed to assessing their whereabouts by reading many different signs in the sea, including even the colour and saltiness of the water in which they were sailing. On good days measuring the height of the stars enabled seamen to obtain a fairly accurate estimate of their latitude. This was important to ensure that they caught the easterly trade winds off the Canaries when sailing to America and the westerlies through the Azores when returning to Europe. In addition to assessing latitude, sailors could measure direction, and for a century and a half before the first ocean crossing navigators had benefited from the use of compasses to determine the direction in which they were travelling in relation to the magnetic north. A compass, however, gave no clue as to the distances they had covered or the longitude they had reached. Distance had to be measured with a log thrown over the stern of the vessel and tied to a knotted rope that was fed out in a timed rhythm to obtain a rough estimate of the ship's speed relative to the surrounding water. Columbus thus knew in which direction he was going, and he knew roughly in which latitude he could be certain of finding winds to come back again, but he was only partially informed about his daily sailing distances and therefore about the longitude he had reached when he sighted the Caribbean islands in August 1492.

An important scientific branch of navigation that derived from astronomical measurements and observations at sea was the drawing of maps and charts that outlined the shores of the Old World and the islands beyond. Madeira had been noted on fourteenth-century charts and even the small desert rocks to the south of the island had been accurately plotted as an aid to mariners. By 1375 the Jewish cartographer Abraham Cresque, probably working with other scholars in Catalonia and its offshore islands of Majorca and Minorca, had produced a comprehensive atlas of the known shores and tides of the Atlantic and its islands. Maps and charts were copied and sold to merchants and mariners in the ports of Italy and Flanders as well as those of Spain and Portugal. Prince Henry of Portugal's personal collection may have been rather lean and the idea that his castle of Sagres, in the Algarve, had a map room and a team of astronomers and cartographers is probably one of the more enduring myths of Atlantic historiography, but Columbus did acquire a valuable set of navigational charts during his long years of service in Genoa, Portugal and Castile. Such maps helped the hard-headed merchants of Lisbon and Seville, with whom Columbus fraternised over many years, to open the sea-lanes through the Atlantic. It was they, with a little help from Queen Isabella of Castile, who financed Columbus's first exploratory voyage of 1492 and then put substantial investment behind his second voyage in the following year.

The first Castilian settlers in the New World arrived on the great Caribbean island of Hispaniola, also called Santo Domingo and later split into Haiti and the Dominican Republic, on Columbus's second voyage. The first voyage had demonstrated – at the cost of one shipwreck and the loss of all those who had been left behind in the Caribbean for want of sufficient return berths on two small surviving caravels – that travel to and from a new set of Atlantic islands was feasible. The second voyage, consisting of seventeen vessels, was bursting with colonial optimism. The settlers were inspired not so much by the earlier colonisation of the sugar islands in the eastern Atlantic as by the great discoveries of gold recently made on the African mainland. Columbus knew the sugar islands well, having lived on Madeira, but he also knew about the gold trade and may have visited the trading fortress of Elmina while working for the Portuguese royal house as one of its many Genoese sea captains. That supply of gold from Africa had proved reliable and plentiful since 1471 and Spaniards were profoundly anxious to find comparable mines of their own. Many of the Castilians who accompanied Columbus to the new 'paradise' that he claimed to have discovered were interested neither in planting sugar nor in trading coloured cloth for grains of gold dust, but in the booty to be won by plunder. They had been accustomed to a life of frontier warfare. In Spain the plundering of neighbours had taken on a new vitality in early 1492 when the current truce between Christian Castile and Muslim Granada was broken by the forces of Christendom and the last Muslim rulers in Western Europe were driven to seek refuge in Morocco. The pillaging of Granada had been the last opportunity for crusading plunder and some of those who failed to make rich pickings may have been tempted to seek their fortune on the new islands of the far Atlantic shore. They did not make disciplined colonists.

Two models dominated the first generation of Spanish colonial ideology once the Caribbean had been 'discovered'. The Castilian crown wanted a peaceful colonising model taken from the sugar islands.

Queen Isabella's ambition was to create farming communities in which settlers would work in harmony with converted 'Indians' to produce sugar for export and grow crops and livestock for subsistence. The rival model, which inspired Castilians of all ranks and conditions to flock to Hispaniola, was one in which trading factories would be set up and commercial fortunes would be made without the immigrants having to do any manual work. These immigrants hoped to find an American 'Gold Coast', comparable to the coast from which the Portuguese were buying 20,000 ounces of gold each year. They had also been led to believe, thanks to Columbus's absurd boasting, that they would be able to buy pepper that was as good, as plentiful and as cheap as the African pepper recently discovered by the Portuguese. Columbus later tried – unsuccessfully – to defuse the unrealistic visions of Atlantic wealth that he had spawned. Gold, he belatedly pointed out, had to be won by hard work in the mines and pepper grew on trees that had to be tended before the crop could be harvested and dried. Since neither gold nor pepper was produced in the expected quantities, Columbus tried to persuade both the crown of Castile and the settlers of Hispaniola that the real wealth of the 'Indies' lay in the value of its slaves.

Enslavement was the source of much of the grief that befell the first attempt at colonisation on the American islands. When the first sailors and settlers landed their initial craving was for women and the early accounts of the Castilian voyages coyly admit that the men from the Old World were immediately anxious to enslave harems of concubines. The fighting between rival factions of young Castilians was sometimes generated by jealousies over girls and the destruction of the first shipwrecked colony on Hispaniola by the local inhabitants was probably triggered in part by revenge raids over the persistent stealing of women. Despite the atrocities committed by the slave-catchers, Columbus was convinced – by the time he was ready to embark on his third trip to America in 1498 – that the Caribbean could supply Europe with 4000 slaves a year. He tried to persuade Isabella that the disappointing lack of gold could be made good by selling cheap American slaves at a profit of 20 million silver coins a year. He admitted that the first attempts at enslaving Caribbean peoples had led to heavy mortality, but he pointed out that the first shipments of Canary and Guinea slaves to Europe had also suffered heavy losses before the trade settled into a profitable routine. Bringing Native American slaves to Europe, Columbus piously argued, would ensure that they obtained an opportunity to live Christian lives.

Queen Isabella, though herself profoundly pious, was not convinced by her admiral's advocacy of slavery as a method of conversion but Columbus – in his uniquely pig-headed determination to make money – persevered with his slaving designs. When, however, he did actually send slaves rather than pepper and gold to Europe, this initiative overstepped any limits that even his admiring queen was willing to tolerate, and a new colonial envoy who was dispatched to Hispaniola arrested Columbus and sent him back to Seville dressed in prison chains. These chains he theatrically paraded before the court to demonstrate the degree to which he had been wronged by a 'usurper' appointed to take away his rightful and hereditary titles. By this time, however, the reputation of the old Genoese admiral was irretrievably tarnished. The Portuguese, moreover, had dramatically won the race to find the 'real' Indies in the east. Manuel of Portugal now held not only the gold monopoly in Africa but the pepper monopoly in Asia. The whole Genoese community in Castile became the victim of abuse and disdain heaped on it by disappointed Spaniards. Columbus and his family were given one more opportunity to make good their colonial aspirations but the fourth expedition failed as dismally as the third.

After ten years of settler cruelty and violence that inept members of the Columbus family were unable to hold in check, the colonisation of the West Indies settled into a more ordered discipline under royal governors appointed by the crown in place of semi-autonomous lords-proprietor. Nicholas de Ovando, who governed the Spanish West Indies from 1502 to 1509, recognised that in the Caribbean, as in Africa, land was plentiful but people were scarce and that prospective owners of wealth were therefore the owners of people not the owners of land. Instead of providing settlers with grants of empty territory, therefore, future governors of the islands adopted a pattern of colonisation that resembled the one practised on the Canary Islands. The allocation of land-with-peoples was loosely modelled on the thirteenth-century Castilian conquest of Andalusia, the Muslim land of southern Spain. The medieval Castilians, however, had moved from the often cold and rather dry plateau of central Spain to the warm and fertile valleys of southern Spain, whereas the fifteenth-century conquistadores were moving from rich if rather crowded orchards of Andalusia to the considerably less attractive islands on either side of the Atlantic. In so doing, however, the institutional systems for the distribution of land and peoples, the *encomienda* and the *repartimiento*, were retained. Once the indigenous 'enemies' had been defeated and demobilised by the white invaders they and their property were seized and each conquistador was rewarded with a parcel of land and an allocation of 'Indians' assessed according to his social status. In Spain many of the beneficiaries of conquest had belonged to the Christian orders of chivalry that had been mobilised for the assault on Andalusia, but in the Caribbean, as in the Canaries, the economic attractions were not enough to draw in institutional investors or the large land-owners.

Finding gold remained the lasting dream of every settler who left Spain for the Caribbean. In order to do so each one compelled the 'Indians' who had been awarded to him to search the countryside for streams of alluvial gold dust or hills of ore-bearing rock. Colonists came in their thousands hoping to get rich quickly and return to the civilised comforts of Spain. They had little incentive to husband the energies of their workers for long-term gain. They behaved more ruthlessly than slave-owners, who incurred loss and expense when a slave died for lack of care and nutrition and had to be replaced. The Caribbean settlers did not suffer undue remorse if they worked their 'Indian' miners to death. It was the crown that was perturbed by the death rate among allocated 'Indians' and royal officials tried to protect Caribbean peoples for the sake of long-term economic development. Some Christian priests and friars were also exercised about the welfare of their 'native' protégés who were all too frequently brutally mishandled. Despite official policies, and Church sensitivities, the protection of Native Americans largely failed on the Caribbean islands. By the 1530s Spain was so short of colonial subjects in its New World that far from exporting slaves, as Columbus had recommended, it began to import them from the Old World.

If the conquest of Hispaniola had proved to be a disappointment to Castilians, for the Hispaniolans it was a disaster. Had agriculture been adopted as the basis of colonial production the situation might have been different. Hispaniola is very much larger than Tenerife, the soil is more fertile, the rainfall more bountiful and the climate entirely suited to the growing of sugar. When part of the island was later seized by France a new generation of settlers was able to grow so much sugar, admittedly with huge numbers of African slaves, that eighteenth-century Hispaniola became the richest colony on earth. Before that the mindless plundering of Castilian settlers had helped bring about the catastrophic elimination of most of the indigenous population. In addition the introduction of European livestock played havoc with a hitherto flourishing local agriculture. The farmers of Hispaniola had lived reasonably well off crops of maize supplemented with fish and tomatoes, but when settlers introduced pigs and cattle to the islands they roamed freely, trampling the crops and partially destroying the subsistence economy. A combination of dwindling food supplies and excessive labour demands by foreigners brought a decline in nutritional standards until a population weakened by hunger became prone to disease. Miners in cramped and dust-laden conditions died of lung disease, overwork and physical maltreatment by disappointed colonial taskmasters who found the colony's yields of gold insufficient to match their dreams. The culmination of the demographic catastrophe came when epidemics of hitherto unknown diseases swept the mining camps. Measles and smallpox became particularly virulent among populations that had no previous experience of either and therefore had no childhood immunities to protect them. Figures are not available for the pre-conquest population of Hispaniola, but the post-conquest population was quickly reduced to a bare 50,000 people on an island fifty times the size of Madeira.

Labour policy in Hispaniola, as in most colonies, was the most difficult aspect of governance and was the one that caused the greatest disputes between the settlers and their governors. Labour protection laws failed, and when the labour-intensive economic activities of planting and mining ceased to be viable, some settlers became ranchers who did not need many client workers and whose main export became cattle hides. From Hispaniola ranching spread to the adjacent island of Cuba where land was even more plentiful and the local population was even more scarce. Cuba was clearly not, as had once been hoped, an island off the coast of China and the optimistic search for Japanese pagodas had been conducted in vain. As the hide and leather industry spread, however, it began to support a rising number of lesser Castilian gentlemen who preferred the open frontiers of colonial life to the more confined opportunities back in Europe. It was among these gentlemen that the second phase of Castile's transatlantic empire-building took shape in the generation after the death of Columbus's patron-queen in 1504 and of Columbus himself in 1506.

On the American mainland, beyond the Caribbean islands, the Spaniards gradually became aware of a civilisation based on great cities. The most resplendent of these was the city of Mexico, Tenochtitlan. It represented an urban social order and an artistic culture such as the Atlantic colonisers had so far only encountered in

Morocco. Mexico City was built on a network of lakes and canals like Venice, one the richest cities in Europe, or like Jenné, one of the finest cities in Africa. The city was protected by its waterways and enriched by them since the Aztec rulers could bring supplies of grain and cloth into their huge market with canoe transport. The urban complex around the market, the temple and the palace may have exceeded the size and splendour of Seville, the largest city any sixteenth-century Castilian would have seen. The affluence of the ruling aristocracy of Mexico stimulated the city's literature as well as its architecture. Neither, however, was of any interest to the Spaniards who invaded in 1519. Much of the Aztec literature was destroyed as 'heathen' by the first wave of conquistadores, and the great temple of the gods was pulled down and rebuilt in the shape of a Renaissance cathedral of the Mediterranean style. The invaders brought not only their vandalism from the islands to the mainland but their diseases, which quickly decimated the closely packed urban community without even sparing the élite, one of whose kings apparently died of smallpox during the wars. The question that exercises the historian is how was it that a few bands of Spaniards, landing on an open coast 200 miles from the powerful and magnificent lakeside city in the highlands, succeeded in destroying America's most resplendent empire in a matter of three short years?

At least one of the explanations for the fall of Mexico is associated with the bold diplomatic strokes of the conquistador Hernán Cortes who had arrived in the Caribbean in 1504, at the age of nineteen, after abandoning his law studies at Salamanca in Spain. For the next fifteen years he progressed through a minor colonial career as a public notary, municipal office-holder, the owner of an allocation of 'Indians' and secretary to the governor of Cuba, Velázquez. From that position of trusted responsibility he was placed in charge of one of the small expeditions that probed the coast of the American mainland, making contact with the chiefdoms of the Mayas and searching for the fabled but elusive gold that Spain had so conspicuously failed to find on the Caribbean islands. As he set out on his foray Cortes, the long-serving loyal bureaucrat, dropped his allegiance to his governor and adopted another Spanish tradition, that of the lawless colonial rebel. As a rebel Cortes was much more successful than the Spanish brigands who had helped to destroy Columbus's vision of an American paradise. Eluding attempts to call him back, Cortes slipped out of Havana harbour intent on conquering an empire of his own. Such was his success that he founded the 'city' of Vera Cruz on the coast of Mexico and placed it under the direct patronage of the Spanish crown. When a large punitive expedition was sent from Cuba to arrest Cortes, he defeated it and persuaded many of the soldiers pursuing him to join his venture to the interior.

The increased ranks of the Spanish invasion force consisted of a thousand men with a hundred horses and several dozen crossbows and guns. One factor that must be carefully assessed when explaining European colonising activity around the Atlantic is military technology. In the Canaries the invaders had faced an opposition armed with such rudimentary weapons that conquest with iron-tipped spears and lances had been relatively easy. On the African mainland, by contrast, the Europeans' military advantage over their opponents was never more than marginal. In the north the attempted conquest of Morocco eventually failed when cavalry regularly met opposing cavalry in ranked battle. Similarly, in tropical Africa no territorial conquest was possible when landing parties faced disciplined volleys of arrows unleashed by ranks of well-rehearsed bowmen. Even at the end of the sixteenth century, when portable though clumsy firearms began to be sent to Africa, the military successes they achieved remained distinctly limited. In the Americas it was not in the first phase of American colonisation, on the Caribbean islands, that military technology played a significant role, but in the second phase when Spain successfully conquered the American mainland in the 1520s and 1530s. And yet it seems that Cortes's diplomacy was more important than technology in his military campaigns, and the conquest of Mexico was largely achieved by the policy of divide and rule. From the outset Cortes was able to recruit a thousand Native American soldiers to fight alongside his own men. Much more fundamentally he was also able to form and reform alliances with states that had been, or now became, enemies of the Aztec emperors of Mexico. In order to capture the island city the successful Spanish strategy was to build boats with which to ferry troops and allies across the moat-like lake. By 1521 the old Tenochtitlan had fallen and a new colonial city took shape, built on the ruins of the magnificent indigenous tradition of urbanisation.

In 1519 Charles V, the Flemish grandson of Ferdinand of Aragon and Isabella of Castile, was elected emperor of Germany in addition to being king of Spain and master of some of Europe's richest territories in Flanders and Italy. At this time his Castilian possessions in the Atlantic were of insignificant economic importance despite the great excitement that had been caused by the first voyages from the Canaries to the Caribbean. When Charles retired some thirty-five years later, the Americas, and more especially the mainland conquered by Cortés and his contemporaries, were a very visible source of wealth. The transatlantic colonies had become an important destination for emigrants who failed to make their fortunes in the wealthy Habsburg territories of the European heartlands and therefore sought adventure and opportunity in the New World rather than languishing in the sleepy doldrums of Spain. Mexico, in particular, attracted growing numbers of colonists from Spain, and as time went on the immigrants from Europe included women as well as men, so that some of the new generation of American-born colonists were white rather than brown. By the time Charles's son Philip II took over Flanders and Spain – leaving Germany to his uncle – 10 per cent of the revenue that the crown of Castile could raise for its exchequer came from the infant American colonies, even though the promise of golden colonial fortunes continued to be deferred.

Wealth creation in Mexico was slow at first. The glitter of the cities that had been conquered did not last and after the first fruits of plunder had been enjoyed settling down to a regular pattern of productivity proved difficult. The great crises of the mainland, as of the islands, were of disease and demography. In Mexico, as in the Caribbean, a catastrophic demographic collapse followed the white conquest and left large swathes of agricultural country open to immigrant opportunists. The Native American population of Mexico may have amounted to 10 million but disease, warfare and semi-enslavement apparently reduced it to little more than 2 million within a few years of the conquest. Creating an export economy depended at first on foraging for wild produce. As on the Atlantic islands, one of the first commodities to be valued was dye for the European textile industry. Instead of planting woad and indigo, however, Mexico became the world's largest producer of cochineal dye. The red colour came from small beetles that lived on wild cactuses, and the surviving 'Indian' population was driven by the colonisers to scour the countryside picking the beetles off the spiny plants. Cochineal became a major export of Mexico and of Castile's newly conquered world, a source of considerable wealth for the down-to-earth merchants who received it in the city-port of Seville. It did not, however, create employment for immigrants and the new arrivals from the Old World always had one eye open for the golden opportunity, El Dorado. Their search embraced ever wider circles in Florida, California, Texas and Oklahoma, but they only discovered communities of maize farmers living at levels of subsistence that produced no significant surplus of wealth that adventurers might seize and carry away.

Although precious metals did later become Mexico's most important export, the resource that initially attracted migrants from Europe was farm land. The first farmers to make use of the well-watered and fertile land of southern Mexico were the soldiers who had accompanied Cortés on his conquest. Twenty-five-acre plots were given to foot-soldiers and hundred-acre allocations to cavaliers on horseback. When duly rewarded with estates conquistadores with farming skills introduced wheat into the highlands and sugar cane into the lowlands. Spanish settlers brought with them the plough and the yoke to till the soil and haul the harvest. Where necessary they also introduced the system of irrigation perfected on the old Atlantic islands, or adopted traditional American systems of terracing as used by highland farmers on the mountain slopes. The great farms – the *haciendas* – of Spanish America became the backbone of colonial society and provided food for the urban centres of administration where the whitest and most affluent members of colonial society resided.

The problem of Mexican colonial farming, as of most colonial farming, was that of recruiting an adequate supply of labour while at the same time keeping the price of labour down. The demographic decline that had accompanied the Spanish conquest was made worse in 1545–7, and again in 1576–80, by renewed outbreaks of epidemic disease. The available 'Indian' workforce was so far reduced that settlers had to become more efficient in using ploughs and oxen, rather than peasants and hoes, to break their newly allocated land. Twelve thousand arable farms were allocated to immigrants and all of them wanted some 'Indian' farm labour. In order to hold at least a minimal supply of local workers in the neighbourhood of the Spanish *haciendas* a system of 'labour reservations' was created. In an attempt to discourage 'Indians' from fleeing from these reservations each village was given the right to use, if not to own, a modest allocation of land for subsistence farming, for foraging and for fuel-gathering. Subsistence farming on conquered land that was not currently in use was discouraged in order to force 'Indians' to work for whites however low the rewards might be.

Colonisation brought new forms of agriculture, including the planting of sugar, indigo and later tobacco, but the most immediate and dramatic change was in the impact that pastoralism brought to the land and peoples of the mainland colonies. First, sheep were introduced to the abandoned lands around the devastated highland cities. Later, cows, horses, goats, pigs, mules and donkeys were brought across from Cuba and Hispaniola and invaded the 'Indian' farms of the Mexican plateau, reducing many of them to grazing pasture. Although 'Indians' adopted hens or pigs as part of their farming system, livestock never made up for the systematic damage that was done to their customary pattern of production on open smallholdings. The proliferation of cattle first took place on lands that had been cleared by epidemics of human disease and then spread northward. The cowboys who rounded up and branded each season's new stock symbolised the colonial frontier. The herds ranged ever further to graze the remote wastelands and then returned after the harvest to graze the stubble on the white farms. Some of the bullocks were trained as draught oxen to provide wagon transport but the rest supplied meat and hides. For a time leather was the most important export that Mexico sent back to Spain. Beef from the great six thousand-acre ranches could not be exported but became central to the diet for locally born whites, known in the Spanish colonies as creoles. Mixed-race whites, known as mestizos, settled for pig, sheep and goat meat raised on the minor farms. By the early seventeenth century it was estimated that the cattle population of colonial Mexico exceeded 1 million beasts, almost as many as the surviving human population, while the sheep and goat population had reached 8 million.

In contrast to the early ranches the Christian mission stations of Mexico became centres of carefully tended mixed farming. Franciscans, Dominicans and Augustinians arrived in the New World before the growth of the Carmelite and Jesuit missionary movements in the later sixteenth century. Each convent or monastery built up its entourage of 'Indian' farm labourers who were trained to plant vines and orange groves, tend lemon trees and vegetable gardens, and grow the basic crops of maize, beans and European wheat. In the remote monastic communities of the north, stretching towards California, missions provided models of development in which 'Indian' villagers could learn new techniques for building dams and ditches designed to preserve and carry water in arid conditions. In the south the more entrepreneurial missionary orders also established wealthy businesses comprising not only cattle ranches and sugar mills but workshops that sold textiles, clothing, leather and soap.

In the second half of the sixteenth century, as the *hacienda* estates continued to expand, the colonial labour system of the Spanish colonies was transformed. 'Indian' slavery was outlawed, if not quite abolished, and by 1570 Mexico had bought 25,000 black slaves from across the Atlantic. African slaves, however, were expensive and every effort continued to be made to harness local 'Indians' to 'modern' colonial production by incorporating them compulsorily into a monied economy. Instead of offering labour service or farm produce 'Indians' were required to offer their colonial rulers money in the form of a state tax. This taxation was not designed to pay for services but was designed to force subjected peoples to work for foreign colonisers. Choice of employment was thereby denied since the colonisers were the only employers who paid wages in the colonial coin needed to meet tax demands. Even this money tax proved inadequate in satisfying the rising labour demands of settlers, however, and eventually a system of forced labour was imposed on the dwindling population of conquered peoples. Conscription ensured that colonial labour recruiters, and not village elders, should decide who was to be sent off to the farms and ranches, for how long and in which season. The labour system, as in most colonial societies, was one in which the poor subsidised the rich as peasant villages bore the expense of reproducing and training a workforce that colonial enterprises could then seize without cost.

When their prime span of working life was over the migrant workers of early colonial Mexico were dumped back into the peasant sector to be tended in a weakened old age without imposing any burden of cost on former employers. Villages of exhausted migrant workers that no longer had enough young people to be self-sufficient were compelled to use what income they could generate to buy their necessities from the colonial market. Markets opened the way to yet another form of exploitation that spread through the rural communities. It was based on neither taxation nor conscription but on indebtedness. Villages that could not feed themselves in one season had to borrow money for food by mortgaging their workers to colonial moneylenders in advance of the next season. If subsequent crops were poor, the cycle of debt dependence and deprivation bit deeper. The weakest of peasants lost their independence and became sharecropping squatters living on the fringes of the *haciendas* with no security or dignity. Some squatters worked as paupers on their own lost fields.

In Spanish colonial Mexico, as in pre-conquest Aztec Mexico, wealth flowed towards the cities, and more particularly towards Mexico City. Production may have been controlled by estate managers, but profits were creamed off by urban merchants and lawyers. City wholesalers were able to store agricultural surpluses when harvests were plentiful and when farmers were driven to sell their crops at painfully low prices. When harvests were lean, or when stocks were running low at the end of a season, prices rose and the merchants extracted their profits from the hungry. European migrants to Spanish America brought with them the skills, technology and above all the financial acumen to transform the New World and sustain an urban 'civilisation' in which white people could live at a level of cultured affluence that many would not have been able to achieve at home in Castile. Although the merchants commonly complained that the colonies, like many colonies before and since, suffered from a dearth of ready coin, Spanish financiers knew how to conduct their credit transactions with profit. Mexico City became the financial hub of North America.

It was bullion rather than farm produce that ultimately provided the wealth that Spain extracted from its Atlantic empire. Initially the most promising prize had been gold, but much of that was loot stolen from the Native Americans who had extracted and accumulated it over centuries. The prospectors searching for new gold long remained rather disappointed, though one mine was operated by Cortés himself. Far more important than the mining and washing of gold was the discovery and mining of Mexican silver. Some silver had been extracted before the conquest, but the large-scale opening of silver mines was undertaken by Spaniards from the 1530s. During the first decades of production the miners were only able to crush and smelt the highest grades of ore. Yields increased dramatically after 1570, however, when a method of amalgamating silver ore with mercury was developed that enabled a far greater proportion of the silver to be extracted from the rock. The new technology enabled silver production to be immediately enhanced by reprocessing readily available waste from old mine tips. The profits from the recycling of waste could be invested into new, expensive, deep-level mines. These mines, however, needed not only investment capital but a large labour force. Labour, however, had already become scarce in Mexico owing to the demands of colonial farming and the overall decline in population.

The development of the mining industry imposed far-reaching changes on the lifestyles of the conquered populations of Spanish America. The mining of silver became so extensive in the Mexican silver belt that additional labour was constantly in demand. This was particularly true where a scarcity of water meant that water-powered machines could not be used. Even when ox mills could replace human labour for the ore-crushing plants, scarce mine employees still had to be used to nurture the beasts who turned the mills and to harvest the crops of animal fodder. While the Mexican frontier was still being conquered, prisoners could be brought south to the mine belt and enslaved on the pretext that they were 'rebels' against the colony or 'enemies' of the crown. When the wars of conquest ceased to supply slaves, the system of conscription was tightened to require any 'Indian' to serve compulsorily in the mines for a year at a time irrespective of whether it was in his or her economic interest to do so.

Mine-working was laborious. Some of the mines reached a depth of 600 feet and hauling sacks of ore up the steep underground slopes was dangerous. Many miners fell and broke limbs while others died of bronchitic diseases. When the mines filled with water, and the available pumps and pipes could not clear them, porters were charged with hauling the water to the surface in goatskins. Even more dangerous than the silver mines was the poisonous and unstable mercury mine in Peru that supplied Mexico with the mercury needed for silver processing. In the processing industry poisoning by mercury fumes became an occupational hazard for the unskilled refinery workers who kneaded the amalgam of mercury and silver with their feet in the huge refining pans that released toxic vapours. As death rates rose, mine-owners considered buying slaves from Africa but the costs were too high and the life expectancy of tropical slaves in the cold highlands too low to justify the investment. When black slaves were bought by the highland silver industry it was mainly to serve in the higher categories of skilled employment where trained artisans were particularly scarce. By the end of the sixteenth century Africans amounted to 10 per cent of the population of colonial Mexico, though most black people worked on the hot lowland plantations.

Every section of the invaders' colonial society, from governors and judges to farmers and artisans, was affected by the mining industry. At the top the hierarchy the crown tried to keep a tight control over silver production. Royal tax collectors initially expected to receive one-fifth of all precious metal mined in the empire, but they were not able to maintain this high level of taxation on all mining. In the costly process of deep-level silver mining the royal tax had to be lowered to one-tenth, thus allowing mine operators to invest more of their profits in new mine shafts and better refining facilities. Still the colonial rulers earned handsomely from the industry. Since silver mining required costly credit – any operator who sought to equip a refinery probably had to raise a capital sum equivalent to the cost of buying an Atlantic sailing vessel – the colonial bankers similarly gained hugely from credit transactions in the mining business. The silver industry also increased the scale of urbanisation around the mines and so brought yet more profits to the merchants who supplied the towns with meat and grain. As urban employment expanded a mestizo class of middle-level employees, with disposable salaries rather than conscript wages, gained in prominence. Some mestizos, despite prevailing social and legal prejudice against racial mixing, were culturally assimilated into positions of modest comfort and security in the colonial world. Only the conscript workers, riddled with disease and maimed by industrial accidents, saw little benefit from mine employment.

The initial core of Spain's Atlantic empire was Columbus's Caribbean 'paradise' and Cortés's Mexican 'kingdom' but wealth was also drawn from a third colonial complex on the northern mainland of South America. Colombia, known as the New Granada, became the main source of gold in the Spanish empire. The gold was largely alluvial, rather than mined, and was found in warm valleys below the forbidding highland ranges. Because the climate was less harsh than on the high plateaux, it was possible for the gold producers to employ slaves from tropical Africa without too much risk that they would die from exposure to the thin air of the cold mountains. The Colombian port of Cartagena became the most important landing point for African slaves as well as the most important loading harbour for American gold. By the late sixteenth century Spain had outstripped Portugal as Europe's leading importer of newly extracted gold. Portugal, however, made significant profits out of the Spanish gold trade since Spain had no African colonies of its own and had to buy the slaves who worked the gold deposits from the labour depôts on the Portuguese islands off Africa.

Far to the south of Colombia, on the shore of the Pacific Ocean, Spain conquered one more colony that made a significant contribution to the wealth of the Atlantic empire, although not itself lying on the Atlantic rim. This was Peru, which traded with Spain via the

Atlantic shipping convoys that came to Mexico and Colombia. The Spanish colonisation of Peru in the 1530s resembled the conquest of Mexico a decade earlier. The conquistadores who accompanied the Pizarro brothers were more uncouth than the sophisticated Cortés, and their success in destroying the Inca empire with even fewer men and horses than Cortés had commanded was bloody and brutal. They arrived in 1532 at the height of a civil war and the hundred sword-wielding infantry and few dozen cavalry were able to capture one of the feuding royal contenders. They demanded from him a ransom of 'several tons' of gold and silver before cruelly strangling him and forming a new alliance with one of his rivals. Thereafter the Spaniards proved even less able to control their greed and Francisco Pizarro was himself assassinated by a fellow conquistador. The rape of the Inca state, like that of the Aztec state, was accompanied by a demographic implosion as disease spread down the chain of the Andes Mountains and the indigenous population of the conquered territories was reduced to about half a million people.

The craftsmen and artisans of Peru, like all other Native American peoples, had never discovered the African and European arts of smelting by which ores such as copper and iron could be turned into hard metals. They had, however, acquired great skill in finding and using the naturally available soft metals, gold and silver. In Peru gold had long been worked into fine decorative ornaments but these were of little interest to the conquistadores who melted them down and shipped raw bars of gold up the Pacific coast to Panama. From there it was carried overland to the Caribbean and suddenly, thirty years after his death, Columbus's promises of untold wealth from the New World ceased to be illusory. The first flush of gold bullion derived from plunder rather than production. Although the loot of the 1530s brought some instant wealth to the treasury of Charles V, the Indies still remained a minor jewel in his crown. In the 1540s, however, the Spanish Indies acquired a steady economic importance with the discovery of a new silver mine at Potosí in Peru.

This mine transformed the Spanish American empire during the second half of the sixteenth century. White migrants came in increasing numbers to the New World and by the end of the century a quarter of a million Spaniards had crossed the Atlantic. A sprawl of polluted slums in the highlands of Peru became one of the world's largest industrial complexes. Immigrants continued to include many of the semi-persecuted 'New Christians' who had provided early entrepreneurship on the Atlantic islands. Although the amalgamation of the Spanish and Portuguese crowns in 1580 did not legally open the Spanish colonies to Portugal, many Portuguese immigrants nevertheless flocked to Peru. Peru could not use African slaves as miners since the high death rate would have made them prohibitively costly, but it did import slaves as skilled artisans for the colonial workshops, and Lima, the colonial capital of Peru, developed a significant black population supplied by the Portuguese.

The lines of communication between Peru and Spain were long and complex. Consignments of silver were shipped up the Pacific coast to Panama where mules carried them overland to Portobello market on the Caribbean coast. At Portobello the silver was collected by the annual Atlantic fleet that had left Seville the previous year and spent the winter in the Colombian port of Cartagena. This fleet had to contend with the violent climate of the American hurricane season as well as the constant threat of European enemy action, and pestilential tropical diseases often decimated the crews. Once refurbished the fleet loaded Colombia's gold at Cartagena and set off with an escort of six well-armed galleons to collect the silver from Peru at Portobello. It then sailed to Havana's well-protected harbour to try to meet up with the northern fleet. This Mexican fleet had loaded local merchandise at Vera Cruz, together with any transit goods that had come across the Pacific from the Philippines in Spanish Asia. Although the Vera Cruz fleet carried silver, its main capacity was filled with raw materials, notably the 100,000 cattle hides and 2,000 hundredweight of cochineal sent annually to Seville. This fleet, with its two armed galleons, expected to join forces with the more heavily armed Portobello fleet before running the pirate gauntlet back across the Atlantic to Europe. Only once did the Spanish silver fleet fail to get through. That was in 1621 when it was captured in its entirety by the Dutch in a spectacular military and economic coup.

Although Spain was normally successful in protecting its silver fleet, and the port of Seville flourished as the premier city of Castile and the seat of the empire's administration, some of the wealth of the colonies did leak out, despite the complex web of bureaucratic controls created by the Habsburgs. By the seventeenth century a clandestine back door to the silver mines of Peru had been unofficially opened in the South Atlantic and named the Rio de la Plata, the river of silver. The river provided a route by which Peru could import contraband goods for its markets and could attempt to sell silver without the rigorous controls imposed by tax inspectors. Some of the slaves who arrived Peru from Portuguese Africa came up the river from the south, and some of the silver that was smuggled out of Peru reached the Portuguese in Brazil. This silver stimulated the Portuguese to search their colonies on both sides of the South Atlantic for possible mines.

The wealth of Spanish America had deep and growing repercussions in Europe. The first Spanish migrants to the New World had come predominantly from Andalusia, but as the colonies became more established, and more prosperous, people from Castile, and even Leon, joined those from the south-west in growing numbers. America began to compete with Italy and the Netherlands as a promising destination for would-be Spanish emigrants. Although peasants could not generally afford the transatlantic fares, and noblemen often preferred to stay in the European dominions, townsmen were readily attracted to the New World. By 1574 121 towns had been given their constitutional charters in the American colonies. Towns created employment for graduates in both civil and ecclesiastical administration and for artisans in all the service industries. Towns also created opportunities for servants who followed their masters to the New World and discovered that social mobility was possible and escape from domestic servitude was an option. Some former servants became overseers with power over cringing workers less fortunate than themselves. By 1600 the number of towns, and the number of immigrants, had almost doubled in a quarter of a century of rapid urban growth.

In order to gain permission to sail to the Indies Spanish migrants had to show, on paper at least, that they were not Romanies, Protestants, Jews or Moors. Increasingly those who applied to emigrate did so after receiving reports from friends or relatives on the opportunities to be found in the colonies. The networks of advice and support clustered around particular towns and in the peak years of Spanish emigration, from 1560 to 1579, half of all the men and women who sailed for America were the citizens of only thirty-nine localities. Communities planned their strategies for leaving Europe and settling in America and whole family groups, complete with their retainers, began to take part in the demographic flow, thereby slightly reducing the heavy preponderance of male migrants. Even at the end of the sixteenth century, however, the proportion of women among Spanish migrants had only risen from one-tenth to one-quarter of each cohort. Most men who went to the colonies still expected to co-opt their sexual partners, or even their church brides, among the 'Indian' or mestizo populations, though how far such a prospect was an incentive or a disincentive to emigration is not spelt out. In the latter part of the sixteenth century the white population of Spanish America reached a quarter of a million people. The scale of white immigration, and the frenzy with which new towns were established, continued until the 1620s. Thereafter, however, the number of black Africans reaching Spanish America as slaves began to exceed the number of white Europeans arriving as free immigrants. These black migrants came from the Portuguese colonies in the South Atlantic and it is their experience that forms the fourth part of this study.

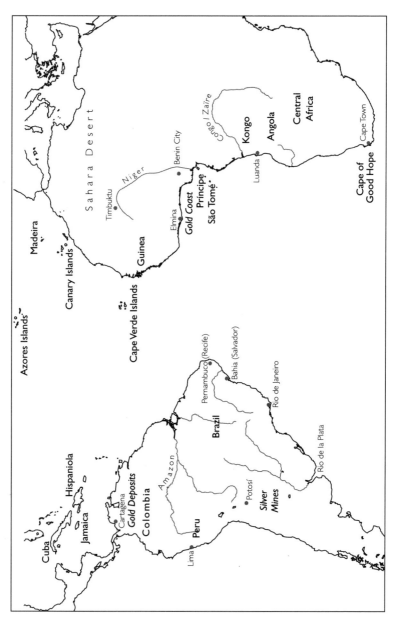

Map 4 The South Atlantic

CHAPTER FOUR

Portugal and the South Atlantic

The establishment of a Portuguese colony in America was slow to take root. In 1500 Alvaro Cabral had set out in the footsteps of Vasco da Gama to lead the second Portuguese voyage down the Atlantic and around the Cape to India. To find the most favourable winds and currents, he had circled in a south-westerly direction and so had unexpectedly sighted land, the island of the True Cross, as he called it. This later turned out to be part of a southern continent, South America, named after the Italian chronicler and explorer 'Amerigo' Vespucci. Cabral's successors in the much larger vessels that opened up the regular Atlantic route to Asia showed little interest in his accidental discovery. Brazil, as the land was later called, fell on the Portuguese side of the Tordesillas line of demarcation that had been agreed between Portugal and Castile in 1494 but the Portuguese had other priorities and it was the French who first visited Brazil regularly. The main colonial activity was logging, and the territory was named after the brazilwood dye that was extracted from tropical timbers. As in so many early Atlantic colonies it was the European textile industry that created a demand for exotic produce, purple orchilla dye from the Canaries, indigo from the Cape Verdes, cochineal from Mexico and redwood dyes from Brazil. For thirty years, however, Brazil remained the backwater of the Atlantic empires.

The delayed rise of Brazil as an influential colonial power was very much slower than the economic rise of Mexico. Several reasons explain the difference. In the first place silver mines had been discovered in Mexico by the 1550s and they attracted large-scale immigration and generated wealth that fuelled the wider agrarian and urban economy of the colony. In Brazil mining only became a prosperous sector of production in the 1690s with the discovery of gold, and later diamonds. The second reason for the slow growth of Brazil was the limited scope for incorporating local peoples into the colonial production process. In Mexico many of the 'Indians' died as a result of colonisation, but those who survived were probably more numerous, or at least more concentrated, than the scattered indigenous peoples of Brazil. The demographic weakness of Portuguese America was accentuated by the demographic weakness of Portugal itself. Portugal and Madeira had little more than a million people upon whom to draw for American colonial settlers compared to the 8 million in Spain and the Canaries. When Brazil began to diversify its colonial activity beyond rudimentary trading in shoreline factories it eventually became, albeit very slowly, more dependent than Mexico was on the importation of slaves from Africa. Even when slaves had become available to prospective Brazilian planters, the Portuguese empire in America remained frail when compared to the Portuguese empire in Asia. Shortly before the end of the sixteenth century the India trade, though under threat from several rivals, still contributed ten times more to the imperial exchequer of Portugal than did burgeoning Brazil, which supplied only 2 per cent of the king's revenues. Not until the seventeenth century did Brazil begin to prosper.

The first attempts to extract revenue from Brazil had been distressingly similar to those used elsewhere in the Atlantic world. In 1511 a Florentine merchant who traded Madeira sugar in Lisbon sent a small boat to Brazil to buy 5,000 logs of brazilwood in exchange for metal tools that had hitherto been unknown to indigenous Brazilians. The crew of this boat made their bounty on the voyage by bringing back thirty-five Tupi-speaking Brazilians whom they had cruelly enslaved in the way that Columbus and his men had enslaved Caribbean peoples twenty years earlier. Much of the casual Brazil trade, conducted through African-style factories, did not originate among Italian merchants of Lisbon, but linked South America to France. The kings of France refused to recognise the monopolistic rights that popes had granted to Spaniards and Portuguese trading to the New World. Even more subversively many of the French merchants came from La Rochelle and were Protestant Huguenots who did not belong to the Catholic Church and did not accept the pope's jurisdiction. It was not until the 1530s, thirty years after Cabral had first sighted the country from a Portuguese ship, that John III of Portugal began to initiate a systematic colonising policy in Brazil. He adopted the Spanish custom of giving land grants to enterprising and educated members of his courtly entourage in the hope that they would take the initiative in making Brazil both culturally Portuguese and economically prosperous. A dozen lords-proprietor were given hereditary captaincies but they failed to attract either settlers or investments and only two of the new colonial provinces showed any sign of success. In the case of Bahia, however, the whole settlement was burnt down in a war with a neighbouring village. Elsewhere neglect rather than violence was the cause of colonial failure.

Despite the setbacks, logging onshore and whale-hunting offshore were gradually replaced by agriculture as the basis of Portugal's interest in its huge but empty South American dependency. The huge hinterland was scarcely explored before the seventeenth century. Some European livestock was introduced and, as in the early Caribbean, a cattle industry took root which supplied settlers with oxen for transport and merchants with hides for export. The indigenous crops of the American tropics, notably cotton and later tobacco, were tried at various times in Brazil's history with a greater or lesser degree of success. But the most lasting agricultural results were obtained by the introduction of sugar-cane from the colonial islands of the eastern Atlantic. Brazil had two very large natural harbours, Bahia (now Salvador) and Rio de Janeiro, which provided shelter along the east coast and in time became focal points for immigrant colonisation. The first major settlement, however, was in the north-east at Pernambuco (now Recife), which had the advantage of being a thousand miles closer to Europe than Rio de Janeiro. West of Pernambuco the tropical north coast of Brazil stretched out a thousand miles towards the Amazon and where conditions seemed propitious small sugar settlements were planted along the creeks.

Colonial change came to Brazil, as elsewhere in the Atlantic, in the 1550s as the power of the royal rulers of Europe began to grow. In Brazil the era of private initiative and conquest had lasted, as in the cases of Mexico and Peru, little more than a dozen years. A centralisation of authority in the colonies reflected the emergence of more powerful institutions of administration in Europe. Shortly before the appointment of the first governor-general for Brazil, for instance, the Portuguese crown had established a reformed inquisition as the powerful tribunal used to maintain social control over Portugal itself. Although no such tribunal was introduced into Brazil, the authoritarianism that it represented did take root in the empire. The rise of more effective and centralised government coincided with new Portuguese visions of opportunity in the Atlantic empire. The realisation that Peru, on the Spanish side of South America, possessed mines of silver naturally stimulated interest in Brazil's potential. At the same time the need for new land on which to grow sugar was being felt as the Portuguese island colonies became crowded. An even more important threat to Portugal's hitherto abundant colonial wealth came with the first signs that the pepper trade from India was under threat and that Venice, using the Ottoman land routes through Egypt and Syria, was beginning to compete effectively with Portugal's sea route to Asia. Under these circumstances John III of Portugal took a direct hand in enhancing his colonial empire and appointed a governor-general to rule over the whole subcontinent of Brazil. The first holder of the post was given the apparently mundane tasks of rebuilding the ramshackle settlement of Bahia with stones and mortar. From the new capital on the great bay his authority would then stretch out to offer military protection for the future sugar mills of the coastlands.

In Brazil, as in the Spanish empire, the central issue in founding a colonial plantation system was the problem of finding a competent and reliable labour force. Portugal tried to follow a similar path to that of Spain in order to cajole and coerce the 'Indians' of South America into working for foreign settlers. Native Brazilians were naturally reluctant to lose their economic freedom and were therefore accused of being enemies of the invaders. Colonial governors decided that it was legitimate to attack and enslave anyone who resisted them and Brazilian colonisation progressed in the manner adopted on the Canary Islands fifty years earlier. Unless severely provoked, however, most Brazilians were not war-like and finding a morally acceptable excuse for enslaving them often proved difficult. A more peaceful policy of transforming 'Indians' from self-reliant maize-and-cassava farmers into obedient colonial labourers was therefore tried. The experimental labour policy was entrusted to a newly established missionary order, the Jesuits.

The Society of Jesus became one of the key institutions that helped to revitalise the Portuguese empire after the first flush of success in Africa and India. The Jesuit fathers combined the two roles of proselytising and colonising. Their order had been established in 1540 as the innovative arm of a counter-reformation that aspired to invigorate the Catholic Church after the great losses it had suffered as a result of Protestant separatism. In Portugal the Jesuits were given responsibilities in the field of education and had founded a university. In Asia they took on extensive missionary work as far afield as Japan. In Africa and Brazil they took a leading role in creating colonies that were politically and economically viable and in which they hoped that Christianity would take root.

By the end of the sixteenth century more than 100 Jesuit priests had been sent to Brazil to try to indoctrinate local peoples into accepting Christian 'civilisation' together with all the social and economic consequences that this might entail in a colonial setting. The success rate was not encouraging and many of the mission fathers had a low opinion of the men and women whom they tried to bring into the fold of their village compounds. Their task was not made lighter by the hostility of Brazil's first bishop, appointed to the new see of Bahia in 1551. In the stifling atmosphere of a colonial backwater quarrels between expatriates became running sores of great virulence. The irascible bishop was pitted not only against the Jesuits but against the governor. He was eventually recalled, though he died after being shipwrecked on his way home, and his successor established better working relations with the civil authorities. The next governor, Mem de Sá, ruled Brazil for fifteen years and gave his full support to the Jesuit policy of bringing colonised subjects into controlled villages. More than 30,000 Native Brazilians were quickly enrolled in the Jesuit homesteads. Independent-spirited peasants who refused to comply with an order to move into a Jesuit compound could be deemed 'warlike' and captured for slave duties in the sugar fields. Once enrolled in villages or conscripted on plantations, Brazilians, like the clustered 'Indians' of Spain's colonial towns, were prone to suffer from epidemics of smallpox, measles and other hitherto unknown diseases. The political 'success' of colonial villagisation was rapidly followed by demographic failure in the Jesuit communities. Survivors of the epidemics were allocated to the settlers while the dead began to be replaced with slaves from Africa. The slavery that became the basis of Brazilian society over the course of the seventeenth century, and which endured until the end of the nineteenth century, had ancestral roots that were well established in the medieval societies of southern Europe. Before the European slave traders arrived in Africa slavery was a small, but normal, part of daily life in both Portugal and Castile. Until the 1440s slaves were almost universally white and worked alongside free labourers in the most menial forms of employment. But whereas free workers could choose their employer, it was employers who chose which slaves to buy or sell, leaving the slaves themselves few if any basic choices. Although slaves were deemed to be 'property', like barns or horses, they did have some rights, including the right to life, and in some cases slaves were allowed to keep a portion of any money they earned when their services were contracted out by their owners. Women slaves were afforded the same theoretical, though often ineffectual, protection against sexual violence or seduction as other female servants, but only if they were white. When black slaves began to arrive in Europe the women were granted no more protection against male exploitation than were common bawds, and so the racial prejudices that discriminated against black peoples in general, and black slaves in particular, began to be accepted in Europe. In the colonies blackness became ever more closely associated with slavery.

Once discrimination against black slaves had become institutionalised, the treatment of black slaves became harsher. Each time a slave was sold to a new owner he or she was liable to be branded with a hot iron, as was done with cattle. Some owners even put their brand marks on the faces of their slaves so that they were instantly recognisable even when clothed. When slaves failed to obey orders they could be punished without recourse to the courts, and whipping or other forms of torture were practised. Slaves screamed with pain when molten fat was poured over them to humiliate them as a terrifying example to others. An owner who went so far as to injure a slave fatally might occasionally be punished by exile in the fortresses of Morocco until any fine imposed for cruel mistreatment of the slave had been paid. But since a slave, in accordance with old Roman law, owed his or her master 'perpetual service' there was an incentive for the owner to keep the slave in working condition. This meant that slaves in Europe were regularly fed and in some respects had greater security than daylabourers who might only eat adequately on the days when they found employment. Slaves, moreover, could not be threatened with the dreaded exile in Africa since that was where many of them originated and would probably have been pleased to return.

Although slaves were common in the south of both Portugal and Spain, the numbers rarely reached 5 per cent of the population even in the least populated regions newly conquered from their Moorish rulers. In the seaports where many imported slaves were sold to new owners, Africans worked as water-carriers, house-painters, cleaners and occasionally as liveried coachmen. There may have been 30,000 slaves in Portugal by the mid-sixteenth century, and perhaps 100,000 in Spain, far more than in the Atlantic colonies at that time.

Thereafter, the number of slaves arriving in Europe virtually dried up and the existing slaves were slowly absorbed into the mainstream of the population. By the eighteenth century slavery had effectively ended in Europe and as an institution was confined to the colonies. It was there that slavery took on the dimension that became associated with the Atlantic economic system.

Before the seventeenth century, when the scale of Atlantic slaving increased rapidly, the price of slaves remained relatively high. In Africa this price was largely determined not by the costs of transport, or by the profits expected by the shipowners, but by the value put on each slave by the African dealers who sold them. The economic bargaining power of the suppliers was strong when transatlantic colonisers had no other option than to buy foreign workers from Africa. African wholesalers knew their markets and prices intimately and would not sell slaves for anything less than the most fashionable textiles, the most appealing personal ornaments and the most sought-after metal goods and glassware. In later centuries Brazil gained a trading advantage over its rivals by offering great rolls of chewing tobacco, preserved in molasses and wrapped in cowhides, and by shipping kegs of second-class rum in exchange for slaves. Both tobacco and rum were addictive and so helped the slave buyers to consolidate their hold on the market to the detriment of any African supplier of slaves whose economic judgement was clouded by addictive craving.

Once slaves had been bought on the African shore the new seafaring owners incurred the high cost of feeding them on the long Atlantic crossing, and of hiring crews who could not only sail the ships but prevent the 'cargoes' from mounting successful rebellions. The risk of wholesale loss through shipwreck, or partial loss through disease, increased the insurance costs of the slave traders whether they bore these costs themselves or passed them on to the speculators who invested in the business. Once safely across the ocean the enterprising captains had to find an appropriate market where their slaves could either be sold as lots to ready buyers or auctioned individually to the highest bidder after each slave had been ignominiously subjected to medical examination. As in a horse sale a buyer would inspect the slave's teeth to assess the likely number of years of labour he or she might serve. In the case of women the prospect of using them to breed baby slaves apparently played little part in determining the price since slave-drivers commonly deemed it more economic to buy new slaves ready to start work rather than nurture children on the plantations.

Similarly, some buyers deemed it more profitable to work their slaves very hard for a few years, and then replace them when they died of exhaustion, rather than spare them excessive exertions in the hope of gaining one or two more years of service.

Since foreign slaves were expensive in Brazil, indigenous slaves continued to outnumber them until the end of the sixteenth century and probably well into the seventeenth. Bands of armed slave-catchers carrying banners hunted their victims in the backlands of Brazil. Some Brazilian 'Indians' were not captured but were enticed to follow the expeditionary flag with promises of fine clothing and good food on the coast. Once the columns of recruits reached the sugar estates, however, families were broken up and sold as slaves to the highest bidders. Each expedition defrayed its military costs and then shared out the profits. The victims, meanwhile, were put to work on plantations where they suffered the same kind of cruel pressures and unusual punishments as those meted out to slaves in Portugal. The expeditionary commanders, some of them Europeans and others mixed-race Mamelucos, then recruited fresh warriors for yet deeper forays into uncharted raiding grounds. Terror spread through Brazil in ripples and some refugees were alleged to have trekked overland as far as the Amazon forest, more than a thousand miles from their burnt-out homes.

The consolidation of the Portuguese territories in northern Brazil did not immediately drive the French out of southern Brazil, where they had turned their early trading factories into a colony quaintly known as French Antarctica. In 1555 some 600 Frenchmen from Normandy and Brittany sailed for Brazil and set up a 'new commonwealth' with guaranteed Protestant freedoms and toleration for Catholics. The immigrants settled near Rio de Janeiro and made peace with the local 'Indians'. They then appealed to John Calvin, the Protestant leader of the city state of Geneva, to send new recruits to protect their colonising venture from the ire of their ultra-Catholic Portuguese neighbours. The iron convictions of the Calvinists who came to join the French in Brazil made the evolution of an inclusive colonial community difficult and violent theological disputes broke out over such questions as the nature of the Eucharist. In French Brazil, as in Portuguese Bahia, the governor was locked in mortal battle with a determined religious leader. In the French case it was the governor – not the cleric – who abandoned the territory, switching his allegiance to Catholicism as he went. Soon afterwards Bahia was able to mount a military expedition that scattered the French settlements and in 1565 Rio de Janeiro was captured by the Portuguese. A royal town was founded and Salvador Correia de Sá, a relative of the governor of Bahia, was made its captain. The Sá family provided Rio's most distinguished citizens for the next two centuries and it was another Salvador Correia de Sá who in 1648 led the fleet that captured the slaving grounds of Central Africa for Brazil.

Once the French had been driven from Brazil the Portuguese overcame their reluctance to invest people and capital in their American possessions and the sugar industry began to expand. By 1585 Brazil had a white population of nearly 30,000, most of them settled around Pernambuco and Bahia where they owned a hundred sugar mills and produced 80 per cent of the colony's revenue. The planters of Pernambuco demonstrated particular opulence when they came to town accompanied by their retinues. They dressed their women in fashionable finery and eschewed the Brazilian diet of cassava and palm oil in favour of imported wheaten bread and olive oil. Such was their well-being that immigrants began to flow to Brazil not just from the dry provinces of the Portuguese south but from the green farming provinces of northern Portugal. Sugar mills, surrounded by 'Indian' supply villages, were built in the lesser colonial territories of Brazil, some worked by watermills as in Madeira, some by oxen as in Mexico, and some by the terrifying treadmills in which so many Brazilian slaves were forced to run for their lives to keep the crushing plants revolving throughout the hours of daylight. Each mill became the hub of a plantation society with its own distinctive culture and its hierarchy of precedence between the various levels of personal servants, houseslaves, refinery artisans, mill mechanics and farmhands who planted, weeded and cut the cane fields. Class relations were rigidly maintained in sixteenth-century style, but colour bars had to be bent to accommodate practical and economic requirements. As in Spanish America some members of the artisan class were slaves who were permitted to retain part of their earnings and so climb the ladder of material wealth and mitigate some of the burdens of social ostracism.

The predominance of males among the free immigrants, as among the bought slaves, meant that women became particularly prized possessions in Brazil. One of the constant crises of Brazilian slave society, as of other slave societies, was the lack of protection that law or custom gave to the modesty or virtue of slave women. A similar darkness sometimes also overshadowed the lives of slave boys who were occasionally raped by their elders. Slave girls in Brazil, sometimes willingly but often unwillingly, frequently had to bear the children of their owners. On the plantations the sons and heirs of planters were normally nurtured by black mothers, or by black wet-nurses when their birth mothers were white. Shades of brown became the normal, occasionally even the preferred, skin tone of Brazilian sweethearts throughout the colonial period. In the tropics Portuguese society was, in this respect, rather different from Spanish society since fewer whites migrated from Portugal to the colonies and whiteness could not be prized as a badge of status among Brazilians in the same way that it was in Mexico. But the racial mixing that occurred should not be interpreted as a colour-blind racial tolerance in the way that Portuguese apologists for colonial exploitation have sometimes tried to pretend. Much of the racial mixing in Brazil was of the violent and abusive kind later to be familiar in the colonies of North America and was practised in the slave pens under cover of darkness. Although 'persons of colour' might subsequently be acknowledged to be of superior status on the farms or in the boudoirs of Brazil, they were not so readily acceptable in the administration or in the Church.

Brazil became the most important colony of black immigrants from Africa during the course of the seventeenth century, but during the sixteenth century the slave population brought from Guinea and Angola, either via the islands of Cape Verde and São Tomé or by direct ocean shipment, remained smaller than either the European or the Native American population. The best guess is that in 1600 some 15,000 of the 50,000 Africans who had been brought to Brazil were still alive and working. As sugar prices increased, and a slave could earn his purchase price in little over a year's work, planters felt able to afford replacements for dead slaves even when mortality rates on their estates rose to 10 per cent each year. The resulting steady influx of new slaves had important social and cultural consequences. Because the slave communities had a low proportion of plantation-born children, the newly imported majority kept alive the musical, artistic and religious traditions of their African childhood. In Brazil society became more African than in any other of the American colonies with the exception of eighteenth-century Haiti. In the hinterland of Pernambuco it was not only the cultural but the political traditions of Africa that were preserved by independent communities of escaped seventeenth-century slaves. Elsewhere aspects of European culture, including Catholicism and modified forms of the Portuguese language, were adopted by Brazilian slaves, though perhaps more slowly than in other slave societies of the Americas.

The early focus of the Atlantic slave supply was the island of São Tomé. It has been estimated that, small though the island was, it may have received some 100,000 slaves over the course of the sixteenth century. As has been seen, some of these slaves were employed on the local sugar estates, while others were sold to the Gold Coast as miners and so remained in Africa though not in their home cultures. A third contingent of slaves was sold to Portugal, some for domestic employment but many more for resale to Spain. Some of the early Atlantic traders, such as the mid-fifteenth-century Cadamosto, noted that the profits from selling slaves to Spain were particularly high. When, from the 1530s, Spain started to buy slaves to repopulate its devastated Caribbean islands the profits rose further. A few years later the demand for slaves in the Colombian goldfields caused prices and profits to rise yet higher. Death rates from lung disease and other ailments in the unhealthy mine camps were costly for the American owners of slaves but were a source of profit for slave merchants who supplied the necessary replacement workers.

The effects of slave-buying on the Atlantic shores of Africa were profound and varied. The first victims of the trade were marginal members of the coastal societies: orphans who had no social patron to protect them, debtors who could not raise the money to repay powerful moneylenders, foreigners who had been captured in war and were deemed more valuable when sold abroad than when put to work at home. As the demand for slaves increased, and the range and quality of goods offered in exchange improved, more people became potential victims. Village magistrates altered the traditional penalties for recognised crimes to penalties of enslavement. As a consequence local rulers responsible for law and order, like state rulers responsible for aggression and defence, acquired a hidden incentive to make decisions that would enhance their earning capacity through the slave trade. As the pressures grew, and social tensions rose, neighbours began to accuse one another of destabilising the community through witchcraft. In an effort to exorcise the evil spirits, alleged witches were condemned to become export slaves. Accusations of witchcraft proliferated and a vicious circle of witch-hunting and slave-selling began to accelerate. Thus it was that by the middle of the sixteenth century the fabric of society had been so weakened in both Guinea and Kongo that widespread violence broke out in the hinterland of the slaving harbours.

In Guinea the wars that erupted after a century of Atlantic slaving were called the Mane Wars. Invaders from the deep interior, possibly from the disintegrating states that had once belonged to the medieval Mali empire, invaded the coastal lands. As they marched through the villages causing death and destruction they swept up the victims of their mayhem for sale to the waiting ships offshore or to the dealers who held them in prison compounds until they could receive a good price for them. The Mane Wars erupted in the 1540s as the new demand for slaves on the far side of the Atlantic outstripped the old demand for slaves in southern Europe. The local communities of Guinea did the best they could to protect themselves by establishing secret societies that sponsored regiments of young men who protected a select few and ransomed their own protégés when they fell into the hands of the slaving captains.

Although no overarching empire was built along the coast of Guinea, the chiefly élite did sometimes co-operate to enhance its own interests. It also connived with the merchant communities to sustain the slave trade and profit from the sale of the powerless. In the creeks and along the estuaries the small communities of European merchants took root and were protected by local aristocracies, to the dismay of the Portuguese crown, which constantly feared that settlers would breach the royal trading monopolies. Diplomatic and commercial ties between the creole settlers and the village chiefs were often cemented by multiple marriage ties. When the Mane Wars were over large merchant families of mixed race and mixed culture became the key slave brokers of the Guinea coast. They also maintained trading links with the official Portuguese colonies on the Cape Verde Islands where similar mixed-race communities, speaking a similar Portuguese patois, flourished on the basis of a growing transatlantic traffic in slaves.

In the Kongo slaving zone the Christianised managers of the king's trade kept at least partial control over the destiny of the kingdom until the late 1560s when the region was torn apart by war, much as Guinea had been twenty years before. The long reign of Afonso had not been one of enduring harmony. The king's foreign scribes and chaplains continued to condone the rising trade in slaves, or even participated in it, despite the king's protests that the business was weakening the social fabric of his realm. Afonso died in 1543, but his immediate successors were initially able to satisfy the rapidly rising pressure on them to supply slaves and to keep their provinces under control. By the end of the 1560s, however, the whole royal slaving structure imploded.

Whether the violence that swept away the king, his courtiers and his business partners was triggered by an internal uprising or by a foreign attack is not entirely clear. The invaders, or rebels, were nicknamed the 'Jaga' and were believed by their enemies, Europeans and Africans alike, to be cannibals. Whether or not they did bond their regiments together through rituals that involved the eating of human flesh, they certainly managed to sow terror through a wide swathe of Central Africa. The king was driven to take refuge on an island in the Congo River that was infested with hippopotamuses while the traders withdrew to their home market on São Tomé. When the traders returned it was with a new colonising agenda, complete with musketeers and conquistadores. By then Portugal was seriously committed to building its Brazilian empire to supplement the dwindling wealth of the old African and Asian empires.

By the 1560s Brazil appeared set to replace both Madeira and São Tomé as the prime source of Portuguese colonial sugar. It was therefore a matter of grave concern that the Jaga War in Kongo had suddenly destroyed one of the most important sources of slaves for the American market. The ensuing panic over the Brazilian labour supply led to the adoption of an entirely new colonial policy in Portugal, one of military aggression rather than commercial and religious diplomacy. In 1569 the Portuguese crown raised an army with which to invade Kongo and restore to its throne a pliant Christian king capable of reopening the great slave fairs and patrolling the land routes to the coast. The first colonial army to disembark in the tropical zone of Atlantic Africa consisted of 600 men. It aspired to pull off the same kind of military miracle in Africa that Cortes had achieved in Mexico fifty years earlier. Some of the expedition's soldiers were armed with arquebuses, which, if not accurate in fire or long in range, were dramatically effective in terrifying an unexpecting enemy by their smoke, noise and occasional deadly success. The captain of the invasion force was Ferdinand de Mello, the governor of São Tomé. He was one of the traders most directly affected by the collapse of the slave markets and therefore most anxious to restore the old Kongo order of government, albeit under Portuguese supervision.

The Portuguese invasion of Kongo expanded and strengthened the expatriate community. Many of the musketeers who put King Alvaro back on the Kongo throne settled in his kingdom, acquired large African families of black wives and brown children and built extensive compounds for their retainers, servants and slaves. They trained skilled commercial agents whom they could trust to lead columns of textile porters into the far interior to buy convicts, prisoners of war and children who had been kidnapped when running errands through the bush. Very soon, however, the Portuguese crown found that although it had succeeded in rebuilding Kongo it had failed to impose any effective control over the returning merchants. The expatriate traders in Kongo, like those in Guinea, had a commercial agenda of their own and did not willingly sustain the exchequer and customs house in Lisbon. Two years after the Kongo king had been restored to his throne Portugal therefore planned to send a second military expedition to Central Africa. This time it decided that instead of working through a tame Christian king, it would adopt the old American policy of granting rights over land and people to a colonial lord-proprietor who would be given the right to conquer a colony but would remain under the sovereign authority of Portugal. The con-quistador who was chosen for this new-style colony in Atlantic Africa was Paulo Dias, grandson of Bartholomew Dias, the sea captain who in 1488 had sailed down the Angolan coast to reach the Cape of Good Hope. The new conquest colony of Angola, like the associated colonies on the opposite shore of the Atlantic in Brazil, became closely connected with the Jesuits.

A preliminary Jesuit mission had arrived in Angola, on the southern border of Kongo, in 1560 as part of the Society of Jesus's drive to establish itself as the Christian arm of imperialism. For the next few years a Jesuit priest was resident at the court of the king of Angola where he was both a royal chaplain and a royal captive. From his rea-sonably comfortable quarters in the palace compound he was able to correspond with Europe and to advocate the creation of an American-style colony of conquest that would impose a Christian government on the peoples of Central Africa and open the way for both the flag and the cross. The advocates of a colonial invasion, both the theolo-gians and the merchants, went to great lengths to exaggerate the wealth that conquest and colonisation would bring to its European sponsors. Whereas the real wealth of the region lay in the value of its slaves, supplemented by the local production of salt, textiles and iron, the colonial propaganda dwelt on the richness of Africa's mines. The cosmographers of the day were convinced that since Angola lay on the same latitude as Peru silver mines were bound to be found there. The Jesuit advocates of conquest connived at such unscientific propaganda and when the charter for conquest was signed in 1571 the Jesuits climbed aboard the venture and claimed their place as the mission force for Africa.

The conquistador of Angola was probably not himself seduced by myths of silver mines in the far interior, though his followers probably were. His own claims were much more down to earth and he aspired to obtain a monopoly on the salt pans of the coast and the salt mines of the interior. He also hoped to be able to build windmills and obtain a medieval-style monopoly on the grinding of corn. Like his Spanish role models, he wished to encourage European migrants to settle in his colony and open the land to export agriculture. His rights to the labour of the native peoples were proclaimed, though the crown probably wanted him to protect its own interests by supplying slaves to Brazil as well as creating a new colony in Africa. Knowing that the most experienced traders in Portugal were ethnic Jews, euphemistically still known as New Christians, Paulo Dias gained a dispensation to take with him six Jewish traders despite any objections that Portugal's newly strengthened inquisition might raise. The Jesuits, who represented the semi-enlightened arm of the reviving Catholic Church rather than its repressive inquisitorial branch, accepted such pragmatism of colonial religious practice.

Whether enlightened or not, the conquerors of Angola and their Jesuit allies had seriously misjudged their opponents. It took months before the invaders were able to cross from a sandy island of Luanda, on which they first landed, to the mainland. By 1575 they began to build a castle but rarely dared venture beyond the range of its guns. The old-established traders of the coast, who had been ferrying slaves to the slave market on São Tomé for almost a century, did not welcome the colonial intrusion that threatened to curb their unofficial commercial freedom. The king of Kongo, nominally an ally of the king of Portugal, was also opposed to the venture and accused the invaders of infringing his sovereign rights over the island of Luanda, if not over the mainland on which the castle was built. Up-country the king of Angola was equally dismayed as he saw more Jesuits arriving, this time with an armed escort. He conscripted royal armies of bowmen who effectively impeded the progress of the conquistadores. The more Angola fought the Portuguese, however, the more convinced the invaders became of the reality of the mythical silver mines that they had been promised.

The Angolan conquistadores failed for the best part of fifty years to make any headway in Africa. Their horses died of tropical fevers, their soldiers feared the volleys arrows unleashed by experienced African archers, their gunpowder was constantly damp in rudimentary earthen redoubts, and their cumbersome matchlocks that were only effective in still, dry weather took ten minutes to clean and reload after every firing. Angola's salt mines proved to be beyond Portuguese military reach and African quarry-masters continued to sell rock salt far and wide into the interior. No mechanical corn mills were ever constructed in Angola and the colonisers became dependent, like everyone else, on local women to pound their grain with heavy pestles in wooden mortars. One far-reaching change that the invaders did bring, however, was a variety of new tropical food crops from Brazil. Over time the local diet of millet came to be supplemented with maize and cassava, both of them crops initially grown to supply the slave ships. The settlers also added pork to the traditional diet of dried fish and salted game. Ultimately, however, the survival of the colonists depended on maintaining reasonably good relations with at least some of the coastal peoples and relying on them for commercial profit, military assistance and herbal remedies in the case of sickness. In dire conditions of dependency the immigrants also needed the best spiritual comforts, and these were not necessarily those provided by the élitist Jesuits. Former Jews established clandestine synagogues in Angola, and some white Christians married into black families and placed themselves under the protection of the local gods and the ancestral shrines of their in-laws.

After 1580, when the Spanish Habsburgs acquired Portugal and its empire, and after 1589, when the lord-proprietor of Angola died still struggling to win control of the captaincy he had been granted, the policy of colonisation by private enterprise was abandoned in Africa as it had been in America. A Habsburg royal governor was sent to secure the toehold that had been won in Angola and to expand the supply of export slaves. A new generation of European mercenaries, supported by a growing number of local allies, expanded the colony by conquering village chiefs and compelling each one to reward his conqueror with gifts, tribute, taxation, food and above all slaves who could be sold to the Brazilian fleets in Luanda harbour. By the late sixteenth century Brazil was buying 3,000 slaves each year from Africa and it is probable that half of them were captured in Angola. This surge in the slave trade increased in the seventeenth century when the advancing conquistadores destroyed first the kingdom of Angola and then the kingdom of Kongo. The number of slaves drained out of

Central Africa by slave raiders eventually rose to some 10,000 a year, leaving swathes of Angola's territory underpopulated.

In the wake of the slave wars the Jesuits stepped up their mission activities in Angola. On the vacated water meadows along the rivers they were able to claim fertile land and establish plantations. With the wealth that they generated the mission fathers bought building plots and – to the envy of their mission rivals – became prosperous urban landlords in the merchant city that grew up around the fortress of Luanda. Although representing the voice of modernity in the Church, the Jesuits nevertheless had to adapt themselves to the labour practices of the colonies, including the practice of slavery. A mission excursion into the interior of Angola required the services of twenty-two slaves, including four litter bearers, two canoe- and two tent-carriers, four carriers for the communion table and its furniture and two more to carry the religious images and the preaching chair for the itinerant priest. On progress through the countryside a mission also required porters for the water, biscuit, slave food, dried fish, wine and vinegar, as well as for pots and pans. Last but not least a trusted bearer was needed to carry gifts to give to the chiefs through whose territory the priest wished to negotiate a trouble-free journey.

Some Jesuits had qualms about the ownership of slaves, despite repeated papal approval of the capture and enslavement of 'pagans', but Jesuits who worked in Angola and Brazil rapidly found that they had little alternative to recruiting the services of slaves since lay brothers were almost impossible to obtain. The Jesuits who planned to build a college in Angola could point to the fact that even in Europe their religious order had used black slaves as workers on the college buildings at Coimbra. Colonial Jesuits therefore accepted slaves as alms or gifts and even traded them as chattels to enhance each religious community's local wealth. Jesuit theologians certified that slavery was being conducted according to accepted moral custom in Angola and that the slaves sent to Cartagena, to work in the Colombian goldfields, would be working under Spanish Catholic authority. Despite the oft-repeated Jesuit approval, when Father Jerónimo Lobo sailed from Luanda to Cartagena on a cargo vessel carrying 800 slaves for the mines, he complained that the wretches in the hold were treated 'as if they were vicious criminals, with no more guilt to justify such treatment, captivity and misery than their colour and our greed' (Alden, 1996. 510).

The image of empire that the colonial rulers of the Atlantic would have liked to bequeath to historians was one in which they had spread the Christian faith to all four corners of the ocean. The reality, however, was that the institution that they spread most effectively and universally among the peoples whom they encountered was slavery. By 1600 churches had been built on both the African and the American sides of the Atlantic and over the following four centuries Christianity did become the most widespread and entrenched religion of both sub-Saharan Africa and Latin America. In the early centuries of imperial aggrandisement, however, Christianity was largely still the religion of traders and conquerors and it only made quite modest advances among the peoples whom the invaders overcame as their influence spread. It was trade and not religion that was the driving force of empire, and by the end of the sixteenth century it had become clear that one of the preconditions of profitable trade in the Atlantic colonies was the institution of slavery. The scale of black slave shipments from Africa still remained relatively small, perhaps smaller than the scale of white migration from Spain, but the scene had been set for three further centuries of intensive transatlantic trading in humans. Some of the men and women who were sold into slavery became Christians, but the spiritual comfort that they derived from their new beliefs was a dubious compensation for the harshness with which slaves were treated either within the bounds of colonial law or, more frighteningly, beyond the bounds of legally accepted practice. In the South Atlantic lawful slavery persisted in Brazil until 1888 and illegal slave trading between Angola and São Tomé was not curtailed until 1910.

Epilogue

After 1600 the old colonial system of the Atlantic underwent fundamental change. The Spaniards and Portuguese were joined by three
new nations – France, England and Holland – all of which added new
concepts of financial and political management to the ideas of empire
and so created a new Atlantic system for the seventeenth century.

The French, who had been driven out of South America in 1565 and
were thereafter preoccupied by a generation of religious war, returned
to the Atlantic in the seventeenth century. Their settlers created a vast
hunting colony in Quebec and spread across America to the shores of
the Pacific. Equally spectacularly, they conquered the western half of
Spanish Hispaniola, Columbus's original island of paradise, and
introduced to it the Brazilian system of slave plantations and sugar
mills. Plantation-owners, and France itself, had gained huge wealth
from sugar by the time Napoleon Bonaparte, the future emperor, married into a West Indian settler family at the end of the eighteenth
century.

The English had begun to seek opportunities in the Atlantic empires
before Queen Elizabeth died in 1603. Semi-official 'pirates' were permitted to raid the Portuguese gold factories of West Africa and the
Spanish silver ports of Central America, and abortive attempts were
made to create tobacco and sugar colonies in both North and South
America. In the seventeenth century these agricultural experiments
eventually succeeded in Virginia and Barbados while self-reliant
colonists created subsistence settlements in New England. By mid-
century the English Republic, under Cromwell, had conquered the
Spanish island of Jamaica and England, like France, established slave
plantations for which it required supply posts on the African side of
the Atlantic.

The Dutch were the most dramatic new participants in the Atlantic
and the ones who did most to stimulate the growth of colonial trade.

The rebel Republic of Holland, and its allies in the United Provinces of the northern Netherlands, pioneered concepts that created a radically new Atlantic system. Instead of initiatives being taken by kings, as in Spain and Portugal, or by individual sea captains, as in the early ventures of France and England, the Dutch created trading companies into which long-term capital was invested by a number of speculators and financial risks were spread over several ventures. The new merchant capitalism of the Dutch republics was as successful in the seventeenth century as the republican banking system of Genoa had been in the fifteenth century. Astute businessmen moved to Amsterdam both from Spanish Flanders, where Protestants were liable to be persecuted however successful their enterprises, and from Portugal, where the leading financiers were frequently suspected by the inquisition of belonging to outlawed Jewish synagogues.

The influx of skill and capital into Amsterdam enabled the seafaring Dutch to put their stamp on the whole of the Atlantic system. They captured the Portuguese sea route to Asia and built a trading castle at Cape Town. They seized the fortress of Elmina and took control of Africa's trade in gold. They crossed the ocean to the Caribbean and in 1621 captured the entire Spanish silver fleet. They conquered Angola and became masters of the slave ports of Central Africa. And they invaded Brazil, capturing the sugar industries of both Pernambuco and Bahia. Only Rio de Janeiro, in the remote south, held out against the might of Holland and fought back to become the queen of the Atlantic seaports.

If Rio de Janeiro became a legendary name to conjure with among romantic white seafarers, it did not have the same resonance among black peoples either in the old Catholic colonies or in the new Protestant ones. The most lasting legacy of Atlantic history was the concept of black slavery. It had developed on the offshore islands of Africa before being carried to the mines and plantations of America. Thereafter, a perception grew, in tandem with the colonial system, that black-skinned peoples were inferior to white-skinned ones. This pervasive idea, rooted in Atlantic experiences, has blighted the history of humanity ever since. Neither the nineteenth-century outlawing of the slave trade and of slavery nor the twentieth-century liberation of the colonial empires from foreign white rule has been able wholly to eradicate racial prejudice among whites or fully to restore cultural pride among blacks. But 500 years after Prince Henry's young hooligans began raiding the shores of Africa, and Christopher Columbus's crazed gold-hunters destroyed the civilisations of the Caribbean, historians have managed to gain a new awareness of Europe's darkest bequest to the peoples of the Atlantic world.

Further reading

Alden, Dauril, *The Making of an Enterprise* (Stanford University Press, 1996) is a meticulous history of the Portuguese Jesuits from which I drew some illuminating detail on the South Atlantic colonies.

Bedini, Silvio A., *The Christopher Columbus Encyclopedia* (Macmillan, 1992) collected two volumes of essays on the early history of the Atlantic by prominent scholars.

Bentley Duncan, T., *Atlantic Islands* (Chicago University Press, 1972) contains an excellent early survey of the Portuguese in Madeira, the Azores and the Cape Verdes.

Bethell, Leslie, 'Colonial Spanish America' and 'Colonial Brazil' (both Cambridge University Press, 1987) are collected chapters from the monumental *Cambridge History of Latin America*. I have borrowed particularly freely from the chapters by Enrique Florescano on Mexican farming, by Peter Bakewell on Spanish American mining, and by H.B. Johnson on the Portuguese in Brazil.

Birmingham, David, *Trade and Conflict in Angola* (Oxford University Press, 1966) examined the wars that supplied some of America's slaves. I have since published some essays on *Portugal and Africa* (Macmillan, 1999).

Boxer, Charles R., *The Portuguese Seaborne Empire* (Hutchinson, 1969) elegantly brought the subject to a wide audience. He refined his interpretations in several challenging collections of essays, *Race Relations in the Portuguese Colonial Empire* (Oxford University Press, 1963), *Portuguese Society in the Tropics* (Wisconsin University Press, 1965), *The Church Militant and Iberian Expansion* (Johns Hopkins University Press, 1978) and others.

Curtin, Philip D., *The Atlantic Slave Trade: A Census* (Wisconsin University Press, 1969) was the first successful scholarly attempts to measure the scale of the Atlantic slave trade and has formed the basis for any subsequent fine-tuning of the statistics.

Davidson, Basil, *Black Mother* (Gollancz, 1961) was one of the earliest and most remarkable histories of the Atlantic societies affected by the slave trade.

Diffie Bailey, W., *Latin-American Civilization* (Stackpole, 1945) is one of the early classics of modern Atlantic history. He also wrote the valuable pamphlet on *Prelude to Empire* (Nebraska University Press, 1960) and (with George D. Winnius) *Foundations of the Portuguese Empire* (Minneapolis University Press, 1977).

Elliott, J.H., *Spain and its World* (Yale University Press, 1989) contains essays by one of the founders of modern Hispanic studies.

Fall, Yoro K., *L'Afrique à la naissance de la Cartographie Mondiale* (Karthala, 1982) sheds fascinating light on the late medieval world of map-making.

Fernández-Armesto, Felipe, *Before Columbus* (Macmillan, 1987) explores the late medieval world of the Mediterranean and Atlantic. It was followed by *Columbus* (Oxford University Press, 1991), one of the convincingly scholarly biographies. He also published *The Canary Islands after the Conquest* (Oxford University Press, 1982), which is a model of colonial historical writing.

Magalhães Godinho, Vitorino, *Os Descobrimentos e a Economia Mundial* (Presença, 2nd edition, 4 vols, 1981) provides an analysis of the Portuguese empire in masterly detail. His *Economia dos Descobrimentos Henriquinas* (Sá da Costa, 1962), which first helped me to rethink the story of Henry the Navigator, was followed by a French volume on the subject, *L'Economie de l'Empire Portugais* (S.E.V. P. E. N., 1969).

Major, R.H., *Prince Henry the Navigator* (Samson Low, 1877) accidentally came to hand and provided an unexpected insight into the Victorian scholarship relating to the period when I was otherwise concentrating on a limited range of very modern reading.

Morison, Samuel Eliot, *Admiral of the Ocean Sea* (Little, Brown, 1942) won the Pulitzer Prize for a reconstruction of the voyages of Christopher Columbus, and its author has been the bitter–sweet hero of scores of revisionist Columbus scholars ever since.

Phillips, William D. and Phillips, Carla Rahn, *The Worlds of Christopher Columbus* (Cambridge University Press, 1992) is a balanced study of a subject on which there are hundreds of books, good, bad and appalling.

Rodney, Walter, *A History of the Upper Guinea Coast* (Oxford University Press, 1970) is the basic analysis from which all subsequent, and sometimes critical, studies of the Portuguese in Guinea begin.

Russell-Wood, A.J.R., *A World on the Move* (Carcanet, 1992) is a splendid introduction to the Portuguese empire by an expert on Brazil. He is now editing a whole library of books on the early empires.

Ryder, Alan, *Benin and the Europeans* (Longman, 1969) has a chapter on early Portuguese diplomacy and commerce in Nigeria.

Sánchez-Albornoz, Nicolás, 'The First Transatlantic Transfer: Spanish Migration to the New World, 1493–1810', in Nicolas Canny (ed.), *Europeans on the Move* (Oxford University Press, 1994) provided me with valuable data on white migration in the Atlantic.

Saunders, A.C. de C.M., *A Social History of Black Slaves and Freedmen in Portugal* (Cambridge University Press, 1982) is essential reading for the background against which the slave empires and black migrations of the Atlantic developed.

Scammell, Geoffrey V., *The World Encompassed* (Methuen, 1981) broke new ground by popularising the wider context of Atlantic history and giving due prominence to all the European nations that participated in its opening. He also published *The First Imperial Age* (Unwin Hyman, 1989) and in a more light-hearted vein edited, for the *Guinness Book of Records*, a volume on *1492, The World Five Hundred Years Ago* (Guinness, 1992).

Solow, Barbara L., *Slavery and the Rise of the Atlantic System* (Cambridge University Press, 1991) contains essays by most of the great names in Atlantic slave history.

Thornton, John, *Africa and Africans in the Making of the Atlantic World* (Cambridge University Press, 1992) restored to prominence the African contribution to Atlantic history. He also published a key study on the *Kingdom of Kongo* (Wisconsin University Press, 1983).

Tracy, James D., *The Rise of Merchant Empires* and *The Political Economy of Merchant Empires* (Cambridge University Press, 1991 and 1992) both contain a wealth of ideas and detailed research by numerous scholars who met together at the University of Minnesota.

Vogt, John, *Portuguese Rule on the Gold Coast* (Georgia University Press, 1979) made a useful foray into the under-utilised Lisbon archives.

Wilks, Ivor, *Forests of Gold* (Ohio University Press, 1993) has an opening chapter that refines the author's forty years of research and thinking about the history of the gold mines of West Africa.

Index